W9-BRG-272

Scott Foresman Reading

Practice Book

Scott Foresman

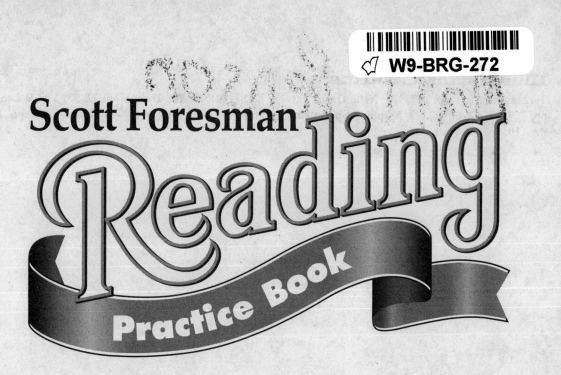

Editorial Offices: Glenview, Illinois • Parsippany, New Jersey • New York, New York
Sales Offices: Parsippany, New Jersey • Duluth, Georgia • Glenview, Illinois
Coppell, Texas • Ontario, California

Illustration Credits

Teresa Anderko: pp. 107, 122; **Nelle Davis:** pp. 12, 72, 82, 112; **Waldo Dunn:** pp. 32, 38; **Vickie Learner:** pp. 2, 7, 28, 62, 68, 88, 92; **Mapping Specialists:** p. 60; **Laurie O'Keefe:** p. 120; **TSI Graphics:** pp. 18, 20, 80, 87, 110; **Jessica Wolk-Stanley:** pp. 70, 77, 108, 132.

ISBN: 0-328-02247-0
ISBN: 0-328-04051-7

Copyright © Pearson Education, Inc.

All Rights Reserved. Printed in the United States of America. The blackline masters in this publication are designed for use with appropriate equipment to reproduce copies for classroom use only. Scott Foresman grants permission to classroom teachers to reproduce from these masters.

10 V011 10 09 08 07 06 05
9 10 V011 10 09 08 07 06 05

Unit 4

From Past to Present

	Comprehension	Vocabulary	Selection Test	Phonics/ Word Study	Research and Study Skills
Ananse's Feast	1, 3, 7	2	5–6	8–9	10
Sam and the Lucky Money	11, 13, 17	12	15–16	18–19	20
Thunder Cake	21, 23, 27	22	25–26	28–29	30
One Grain of Rice	31, 33, 37	32	35–36	38–39	40
The Woman Who Outshone the Sun	41, 43, 47	42	45–46	48–49	50

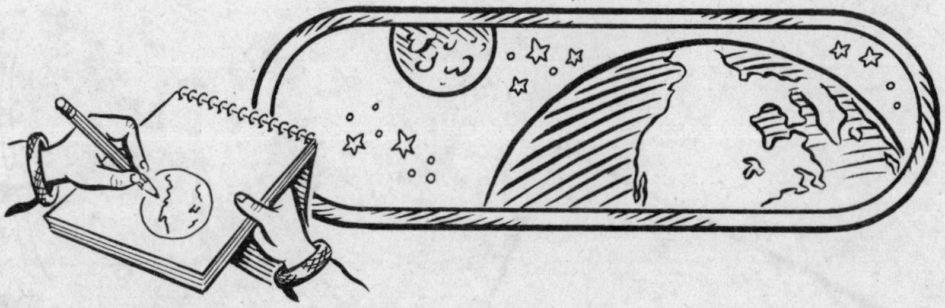

Unit 5

Are We There Yet?

	Comprehension	Vocabulary	Selection Test	Phonics/ Word Study	Research and Study Skills
Flight: The Journey of Charles Lindbergh	51, 53, 57	52	55–56	58–59	60
Chibi: A True Story from Japan	61, 63, 67	62	65–66	68–69	70
Brave Irene	71, 73, 77	72	75–76	78–79	80
More Than Anything Else	81, 83, 87	82	85–86	88–89	90
Leah's Pony	91, 93, 97	92	95–96	98–99	100

Unit 6

Imagination.kids

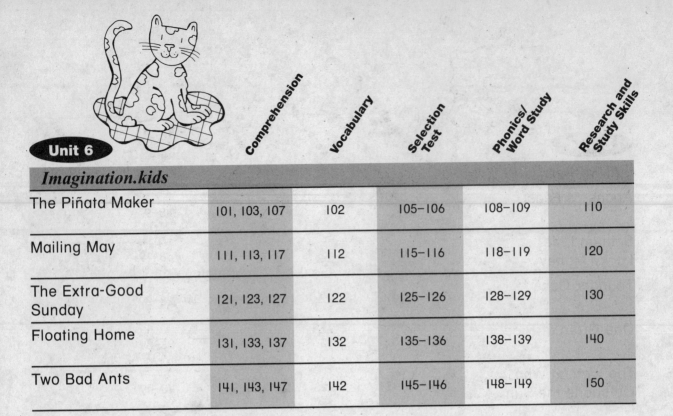

Name Matt Benson

Theme

- The **theme** is the big idea of a story.
- When you read a story, think about what the writer wants you to learn or understand from the story.
- Sometimes you can use your own life to help you understand this theme, or big idea.

Directions: Reread "The Coyote and the Goat." Then complete the table. Use your explanations to help you better understand the theme of the story.

Questions	Explanations
Do you think White Beard thought about how to get out of the well before he jumped in?	1. No because all he was thinking about was getting a drink
What happened that changed how White Beard feels about Coyote?	2. White Beard probably will not trust him anymore
How do you feel about the way that Coyote tricked White Beard?	3. I feel bad that Coyote left White Beard in the well
How would you feel if you were White Beard in the story?	4. I would feel angry at myself because I didn't think before

5. The theme of the story is stated in the last sentence: *The truth hits hardest when it's too late to complain.* Explain what you think this theme means.

____

____

© Scott Foresman 3

Notes for Home: Your child read a story and identified its theme, or big idea. ***Home Activity:*** Read a fairy tale with your child. Talk about the lesson that can be learned from the story.

Name ______________________________

Vocabulary

Directions: Choose a word from the box that best completes each sentence. Write the word on the line to the left.

Check the Words You Know
__ brilliant
__ delighted
__ feast
__ greedy
__ guest
__ stomach

feast **1.** Senai invited all her friends to eat a _____ at her house.

guest **2.** She asked each _____ to bring some food.

delighted **3.** Senai was _____ when they all agreed to come.

brilliant **4.** Senai wanted to look special for her guests, so she wore a dress with _____ golden beads.

stomach **5.** All the food was delicious and by the end of the evening, Senai's _____ was full.

Directions: Draw a line to match each word with its definition.

6. brilliant	a huge meal for many guests
7. delighted	visitor
8. greedy	shiny; sparkling
9. feast	filled with joy
10. guest	wanting a lot of something

Write an Invitation

On a separate sheet of paper, write an invitation to a party. Use as many vocabulary words as you can.

© Scott Foresman 3

Notes for Home: Your child identified and used vocabulary words from *Ananse's Feast.* ***Home Activity:*** Work with your child to write a story about a greedy character. Use as many vocabulary words as possible.

Name ______________________________

Theme

- The **theme** is the big idea of a story.
- When you read a story, think about what the writer wants you to learn or understand from the story.
- Sometimes you can use your own life to help you understand this theme, or big idea.

Directions: Read the part of the story where Ananse the Spider prepares for a feast. Then answer the questions below.

The earth was hot and barren and no one had much to eat except Ananse the Spider. Before the drought clever Ananse had stored away food from his farm, and now he decided to treat himself to a feast.

Ananse shut his door and windows and sealed all the cracks in the walls of his old hut.

"I don't want the delicious smell of my cooking to bring hungry visitors," he muttered.

From ANANSE'S FEAST. Text copyright © 1997 by Tololwa M. Mollel. Illustrations copyright © 1997 by Andrew Glass. Reprinted by permission of Clarion Books/Houghton Mifflin Company. All rights reserved.

1. Why does no one have anything to eat?

____

2. Why does Ananse have food?

____

3. Why does Ananse shut his door and windows and seal the cracks in his wall?

____

4. What do you think someone should do if they have plenty and someone else has nothing?

____

5. On a separate sheet of paper, tell what the theme of the story is. Think about how Ananse and Akye the Turtle behave. Think how you would behave in their places.

© Scott Foresman 3

Notes for Home: Your child identified the theme of the story. ***Home Activity:*** Have your child retell the story of *Ananse's Feast*. Talk about times in your child's life when he or she didn't want to share something.

Name ________________________________

Test-Taking Tips

1. Write your name on the test.
2. Read the directions carefully. Make sure you know exactly what you are supposed to do.
3. Read the question twice. Make sure you understand what the question is asking.
4. Read the answer choices for the question. Eliminate choices that do not make sense.
5. Mark your answer carefully.
6. Check your answer. Make sure that it makes the most sense out of all the answer choices.
7. If you have difficulty answering a question, you may want to go on to the next question. You can come back to difficult questions later.
8. If you finish the test early, go back and check all your answers.

© Scott Foresman 3

Name ___________________________________

Selection Test

Directions: Choose the best answer to each item. Mark the space for the answer you have chosen.

Part 1: Vocabulary

Find the answer choice that means about the same as the underlined word in each sentence.

1. Travis is a <u>greedy</u> dog.
- ⬭ thankful for attention
- ⬭ very skinny
- ⬭ wanting a lot of something
- ⬭ well trained

2. He was eager to fill his <u>stomach</u>.
- ⬭ body part that receives food
- ⬭ large box
- ⬭ body part that breathes
- ⬭ one-room house

3. We invited a <u>guest</u> to lunch.
- ⬭ cowboy
- ⬭ teacher
- ⬭ cook
- ⬭ visitor

4. Everyone went to the <u>feast</u>.
- ⬭ dance
- ⬭ special meal
- ⬭ important game
- ⬭ show or movie

5. Susan was <u>delighted</u>.
- ⬭ embarrassed
- ⬭ very glad
- ⬭ filled with fear
- ⬭ somewhat shy

6. We saw a <u>brilliant</u> star.
- ⬭ very bright
- ⬭ far off
- ⬭ dull
- ⬭ very large

Part 2: Comprehension

Use what you know about the story to answer each item.

7. At the beginning, Akye was—
- ⬭ washing his hands.
- ⬭ swimming in the river.
- ⬭ looking for something to eat.
- ⬭ sleeping in the sun.

8. At first, Ananse did not open his door because he—
- ⬭ hoped his visitor would leave.
- ⬭ was busy setting his table.
- ⬭ did not have food for two.
- ⬭ did not know it was Akye.

© Scott Foresman 3

GO ON

9. Ananse sent Akye to wash his hands because Ananse—
- was worried about Akye's health.
- did not want dirt on the food.
- liked to tell others what to do.
- did not want to share his food.

10. Why were Akye's hands dirty even after he went to the river?
- The river water was not clean.
- He did not wash his hands.
- He walked back through dust.
- Ananse put dirt on them.

11. What happened when the rain came?
- Akye went visiting.
- Ananse held a feast.
- Ananse did not have food.
- Akye was hungry.

12. A theme in this story is—
- tricks are fun for everyone.
- people should wash their hands.
- be careful how you treat others.
- friends always share.

13. Akye asked Ananse to take off his robe because Akye—
- wanted the robe for himself.
- thought it would be fun to trade.
- wanted to make sure Ananse was comfortable.
- knew Ananse could not stay down without it.

14. Both Ananse and Akye pretended to be—
- hungry.
- dirty.
- unhappy with the meal.
- nice to each other.

15. At the end of the story, Ananse probably felt—
- satisfied and thankful.
- hungry and angry.
- happy and playful.
- tired and dirty.

STOP

© Scott Foresman 3

Name ____________________

Compare and Contrast

REVIEW

Directions: Read the story. Then read each question about the story. Choose the best answer to the question. Mark the space for the answer you have chosen.

The Jungle Jamboree

Late last night at the Jungle Jamboree, all the animals joined the fun. The monkeys were there, playing tricks, of course. Everyone ate lots of food, except for the warthogs because they were on a diet. The gazelles and the hyenas were enjoying a great game of tag and wouldn't even stop for dinner. The parrots didn't join the games or jokes; they were happier watching the fun from their seats in the trees.

The animals all sang along to the music, even the shy ones. The lions have terrible voices, but the parrots sing beautifully. The roar of the elephant was heard the loudest, because the monkeys tricked him into singing solo.

1. How are the animals alike?
   - They like music.
   - They like to play tricks.
   - They like games.
   - They eat a lot.

2. The parrots are different from the gazelles because—
   - they sang to the music.
   - they didn't play games.
   - they played tricks.
   - ate everything in sight.

3. The warthogs are different because they—
   - played games.
   - didn't sing.
   - didn't eat much food.
   - ate a lot.

4. How are the gazelles and hyenas alike?
   - They like games.
   - They eat a lot.
   - They play tricks.
   - They sit in the trees.

5. How are the lions different from the parrots?
   - They have bad voices.
   - They like to sing.
   - They like music.
   - They ate a lot.

© Scott Foresman 3

Notes for Home: Your child compared and contrasted characters in a story. ***Home Activity:*** Ask your child to compare and contrast the different members of your family. How are they alike and how are they different?

Name ______________________________

Phonics: Initial and Final Consonant Blends

Directions: Read each word and listen for the underlined consonant blend. Then write two more words that have the same blend in the same place. Underline the blend in each word you write.

1. frighten ______________ ______________
2. best ______________ ______________
3. hand ______________ ______________
4. slide ______________ ______________
5. grin ______________ ______________

Directions: Choose the consonant blend from the box to complete each word. Write the whole word on the line to the left. You will use some blends more than once.

br	st	sl	lt	fr	dr

______________ 6. Danitra had a __omachache.

______________ 7. She'd been to a fea__ and had eaten too much food.

______________ 8. She was __owsy, so she took a nap.

______________ 9. When she woke up, she fe__ much better.

______________ 10. She picked up the phone and called her __iend Sandy.

______________ 11. Danitra invited Sandy to be her gue__ for the night.

______________ 12. Sandy __ought everything she needed for the night.

______________ 13. She had her __eeping bag rolled up tight.

______________ 14. She even packed fresh __uit for snacking.

______________ 15. The two girls slept out under the __ars.

Notes for Home: Your child reviewed words with initial and final consonant blends such as *friend* and *rest*. ***Home Activity:*** Name a word that begins with *fr, st,* or *dr.* Then challenge your child to name other words that begin with the same blend.

© Scott Foresman 3

Name ____________________

Phonics: Digraphs: *th, ch, ph, sh*

REVIEW

Directions: Read each sentence. Say the word with the underlined letters. Choose the word that has the same middle consonant sound as the underlined letters. Mark the space for the answer you have chosen.

1. Stan washed his dog yesterday.
- cleaned
- watched
- fished
- cracked

2. I am still searching for my wallet.
- crouching
- looking
- singing
- wishing

3. Did you hear the telephone ring?
- doorbell
- photo
- nephew
- grape

4. May I have another piece?
- thimble
- alphabet
- winter
- brother

5. Mary brushes her horse.
- grooms
- wishing
- sheds
- other

6. I need to purchase a new coat.
- buy
- chart
- crashes
- attached

7. Mr. Patrick teaches math.
- taught
- stomach
- reaching
- choir

8. I went fishing with my uncle.
- dishes
- short
- watch
- sitting

9. Betty won a tennis trophy.
- trailer
- phone
- wishing
- orphan

10. Greg hugged his mother.
- Mom
- weather
- teacher
- moth

© Scott Foresman 3

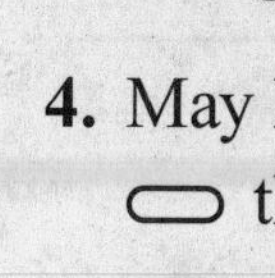

Notes for Home: Your child reviewed words with the consonants *th, ch, ph,* and *sh* in the middle. ***Home Activity:*** Have your child name other words with these pairs of consonants in the middle. Have him or her make four lists—one for each pair of consonants.

Technology: Organize and Present Information

You can use a computer to help you **organize and present information.** A word processing program lets you revise sentences and paragraphs easily. You can also create tables, charts, and even art.

Directions: Read the information about vitamins and think about how you could organize and present it in a report. Then answer the questions below.

Vitamins help a person's body grow and stay healthy.

Vitamin A helps a person resist infections. It can be found in animal fats, such as butter, cheese, and whole milk.

Vitamin B_{12} helps a person develop normal red blood cells. It can be found in liver, kidney, and dairy products.

Vitamin C helps heal wounds or breaks in bones. It can be found in citrus fruits and tomatoes.

Calcium helps bones and teeth develop. It can be found in milk products, dark-green leafy vegetables, broccoli, and tofu.

1. If you were writing a report for class, who would your audience be?

Your audience would be the class

2. What important ideas about vitamins would you want to make sure you included?

Helps develope

3. What headings might you use for a table to present the information above?

4. Why might a table be a good way to present the information above?

5. How are computers helpful for organizing and presenting information?

© Scott Foresman 3

Notes for Home: Your child read information and described how he or she could organize and present it in a report. ***Home Activity:*** Work with your child to organize and present information about your family history that you could share with family members and friends.

Name ______________________________

Setting

- The **setting** is the time and place in which a story happens.
- Look for details or clues that tell you when and where a story takes place.
- Understanding the setting can sometimes help you understand a character's actions.

Directions: Reread "A Hike with Dad." Then complete the table. Answer the first question and give examples from the story that support all the answers.

Questions	Answers	How Do You Know?
Where does the story take place?	1. The story takes place hiking	2. The mountains go on and on
		3. I threw rocks in the river
Does the story take place long ago or in modern times?	modern times	4.
Does the setting affect how the characters act?	yes	The boy begins thinking that they should have set camp elsewhere.
		5.

© Scott Foresman 3

Notes for Home: Your child read a story, identified its setting, and described how it affected the characters. ***Home Activity:*** Before you read a story with your child, have him or her look at the title and the illustrations to try and get a sense of the setting.

Name ______________________

Vocabulary

Directions: Circle the word that has the same or nearly the same meaning as the first word.

1. dragon	pet	friend	monster
2. lucky	fortunate	unlucky	loser
3. scolded	praised	rewarded	blamed
4. startled	pleased	surprised	rushed

Check the Words You Know

__ appreciate
__ dragon
__ lucky
__ rustling
__ scolded
__ startled

Directions: Choose the word from the box that best completes each sentence. Write the word on the line to the left.

rustleng **5.** The only sound was the quiet _____ of the leaves.

startled **6.** We were _____ when a noisy parade suddenly appeared.

dragon **7.** I was almost hit by a float that looked like a horrible _____.

scoled **8.** Mom _____ me for standing in the way.

lucky **9.** It was a _____ thing I didn't get hurt.

apprecite **10.** I always _____ good fortune when it comes my way.

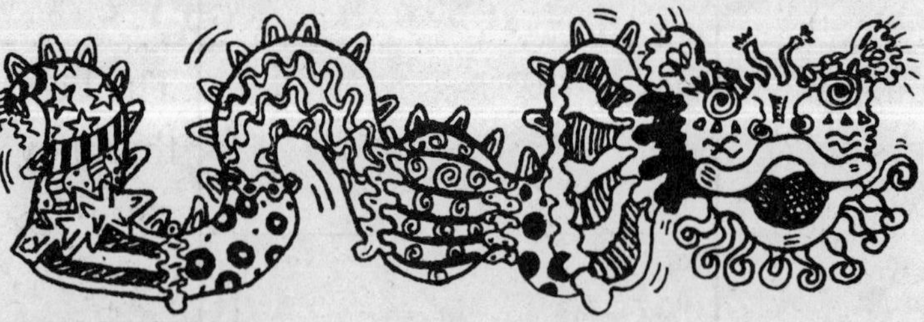

Write a Thank-You Note

On a separate sheet of paper, write a thank-you note for a really nice gift you received. Use as many vocabulary words as you can.

Notes for Home: Your child identified and used vocabulary words from the story *Sam and the Lucky Money.* ***Home Activity:*** Ask your child to tell you a story about a dragon. Encourage your child to use as many vocabulary words as possible.

© Scott Foresman 3

Name ______________________________

Setting

- The **setting** is the time and place in which a story happens.
- Look for details or clues that tell you when and where a story takes place.
- Understanding the setting can sometimes help you understand a character's actions.

Directions: Reread what happens in *Sam and the Lucky Money.* Then answer the questions below.

Suddenly, he heard a noise from outside that sounded like a thousand leaves rustling. He ran to the window to see what was happening.

"Look!" he yelled. Bundles of firecrackers were exploding in the street. Rounding the corner was the festival lion, followed by a band of cymbals and drums. Sam pulled his mother outside.

The colorful lion wove down the street like a giant centipede. Teased by a clown wearing a round mask, it tossed its head up and down.

It came to a halt in front of a meat market, and sniffed a giant leisee that hung in the doorway, along with a bouquet of lettuce leaves. With loud fanfare, the band urged the lion towards its prize.

Text copyright © 1995 by Karen Chinn. Excerpt from SAM AND THE LUCKY MONEY. Reprinted by arrangement with Lee & Low Books, Inc.

1. What does Sam see? ______________________________

____

2. What does Sam hear? ______________________________

____

3. What words would you use to describe the setting? ______________________________

____

4. How do you think the setting makes Sam feel? ______________________________

____

5. Reread the scene where Sam and his mother are walking in the streets on their way shopping. On a separate sheet of paper, describe the setting and how it affects Sam and his mother.

© Scott Foresman 3

Notes for Home: Your child identified the setting in *Sam and the Lucky Money. **Home Activity:*** Work with your child to identify the setting in a book or poem you've read together. Help your child draw a picture of the setting.

Test-Taking Tips

1. Write your name on the test.
2. Read the directions carefully. Make sure you know exactly what you are supposed to do.
3. Read the question twice. Make sure you understand what the question is asking.
4. Read the answer choices for the question. Eliminate choices that do not make sense.
5. Mark your answer carefully.
6. Check your answer. Make sure that it makes the most sense out of all the answer choices.
7. If you have difficulty answering a question, you may want to go on to the next question. You can come back to difficult questions later.
8. If you finish the test early, go back and check all your answers.

© Scott Foresman 3

Selection Test

Directions: Choose the best answer to each item. Mark the space for the answer you have chosen.

Part 1: Vocabulary

Find the answer choice that means about the same as the underlined word in each sentence.

1. We heard the papers rustling.
- crying
- falling to the ground
- yelling
- making a light, soft sound

2. Your cat is very lucky.
- quick on its feet
- sad; lonely
- having good fortune
- hungry; weak

3. James was startled.
- pleased
- surprised
- excited
- remembered kindly

4. The cook scolded us.
- spoke to with angry words
- talked quietly to
- gave food to
- put to work

5. Mark will appreciate the gift.
- be thankful for
- trade for
- look everywhere for
- hope for

6. This book is about a dragon.
- a horse with wings
- a make-believe animal
- a mean witch
- a large, powerful man

Part 2: Comprehension

Use what you know about the story to answer each item.

7. The setting of this story is—
- Chinatown.
- Sam's home.
- China.
- the zoo.

8. Sam receives *leisees* for—
- Christmas.
- the Chinese New Year.
- the Fourth of July.
- his birthday.

© Scott Foresman 3

GO ON

9. At what time of year does this story take place?
- winter
- spring
- summer
- fall

10. In the beginning, Sam and his mother are in a hurry because they—
- want to get the best oranges.
- do not want to miss the lion.
- are hungry for sweets.
- are late for dinner.

11. What can you tell about the old man sitting against the wall?
- He works in a store.
- He is very sick.
- He likes the parade.
- He is homeless.

12. How does Sam feel when he leaves the toy store?
- pleased
- excited
- worried
- upset

13. What does Sam do with his lucky money?
- He buys sweet pastries.
- He buys a new basketball.
- He gives it to the old man.
- He gives it to his mother.

14. Why does Sam's mother squeeze his hand after he uses the lucky money?
- She is embarrassed.
- She is frightened.
- She is proud of him.
- She feels sorry for him.

15. Why did Sam decide at the end that he was "the lucky one"?
- He was better off than the old man.
- He got to see the lion.
- He had made a new friend.
- He still had four dollars in his pocket.

STOP

© Scott Foresman 3

Name ______________________________

Plot and Character

REVIEW

Directions: Read the story. Then read each question about the story. Choose the best answer to the question. Mark the space for the answer you have chosen.

The Canal Street Club

Ming, Steve, and Kim are in the Canal Street Club. They help Mrs. Chen make sandwiches for people who are hungry. Last Saturday was the Chinese New Year so they worked extra hard to make some people's holiday a little better.

They made sandwiches all morning. They had about half of them done. Then they went to help Mrs. Chen decorate for the party. When they returned, they were surprised to see that all the sandwiches were made.

Three young people their age were walking towards them. One boy said, "We just moved here. We hope you don't mind that we made the rest of the sandwiches. We like to help out."

Now the Canal Street Club had six members and the projects went much faster.

1. Who is the story about?
- Mrs. Chen
- the neighborhood
- The Canal Street Club
- the new neighbors

2. The characters in the story are—
- lazy and selfish.
- helpful and hardworking.
- noisy and rude.
- hurried and clumsy.

3. In the beginning of the story, the children—
- meet their neighbors.
- help Mrs. Chen decorate.
- celebrate the New Year.
- start making sandwiches.

4. In the middle of the story, Ming, Steve, and Kim—
- find all the sandwiches made.
- meet Mrs. Chen.
- work on new projects.
- invite new neighbors to join the club.

5. What happens at the end of the story?
- Ming, Steve, and Kim help Mrs. Chen.
- They all make sandwiches.
- The new neighbors join the club.
- The new neighbors finish making the sandwiches.

Notes for Home: Your child read a story and identified both the characters and plot in the story. ***Home Activity:*** Have your child write a story about a time he or she helped someone out. Encourage your child to include a beginning, middle, and end in the story.

© Scott Foresman 3

Name ________________________________

Phonics: Three-Letter Blends

Directions: Read the story. Underline the words with three-letter blends, such as **strong** and **thread.** Then write the underlined words on the lines.

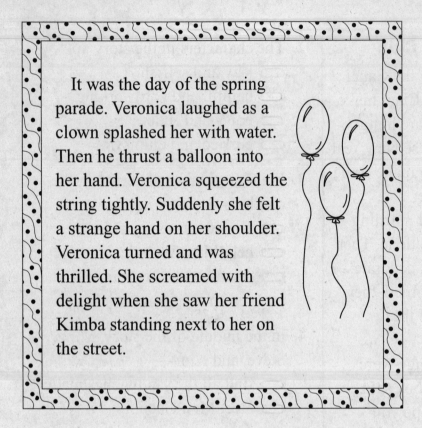

It was the day of the spring parade. Veronica laughed as a clown splashed her with water. Then he thrust a balloon into her hand. Veronica squeezed the string tightly. Suddenly she felt a strange hand on her shoulder. Veronica turned and was thrilled. She screamed with delight when she saw her friend Kimba standing next to her on the street.

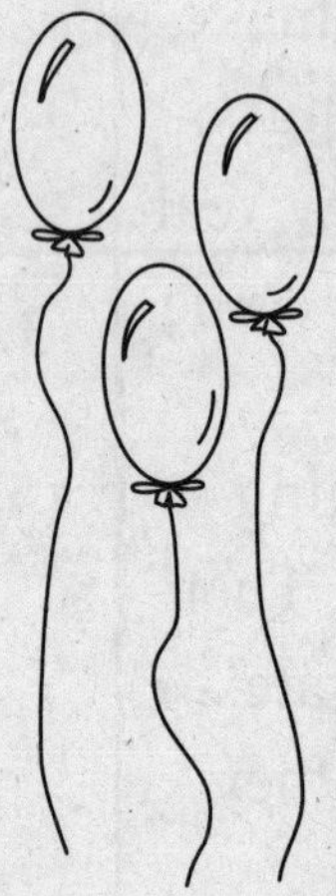

1. ____________
2. ____________
3. ____________
4. ____________
5. ____________
6. ____________
7. ____________
8. ____________
9. ____________

Directions: Read each word and listen for the three-letter blend. Then write three more words that have the same blend in the same place. Underline the blend in each word you write.

10. straw ____________ ____________ ____________

11. three ____________ ____________ ____________

12. spring ____________ ____________ ____________

13. splint ____________ ____________ ____________

14. squeak ____________ ____________ ____________

15. scrunch ____________ ____________ ____________

© Scott Foresman 3

Notes for Home: Your child reviewed words with three-letter blends, such as *str, thr, spr, spl, squ,* and *scr.* ***Home Activity:*** Challenge your child to name some more words with three-letter blends. You can use a dictionary to find words with these blends.

Phonics: Consonant Blends

REVIEW

Directions: Read each sentence. Say the underlined word. Choose the word that has the same initial or final consonant blend sound. Mark the space for the answer you have chosen.

1. Joshua banged on the drums.
- trees
- driver
- daisy
- thousand

2. The baby grabbed my hand.
- happy
- shirt
- blind
- hamper

3. It is very crowded in this room.
- stuffy
- careful
- frowned
- crib

4. I meant to send you this note.
- bent
- measure
- bring
- manners

5. The light was gleaming brightly.
- graph
- shiny
- glitter
- giant

6. I put a penny in my piggy bank.
- bread
- trunk
- bang
- like

7. That clown has a big, red nose.
- crowd
- flower
- clue
- can

8. I need a mask for my costume.
- must
- mark
- small
- risk

9. Aunt Gert scolded Ben.
- scary
- yelled
- praised
- sell

10. The crow gave a loud *caw.*
- train
- crash
- camp
- clap

© Scott Foresman 3

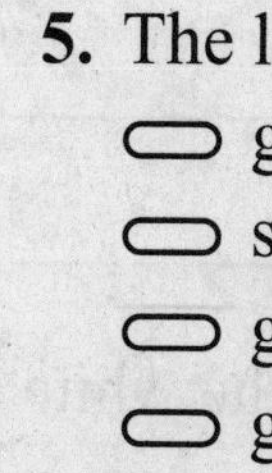

Notes for Home: Your child reviewed words that begin with the consonant blends *dr, cr, gl, sc,* and *cl* and end with the consonant blends *nd, nt,* and *nk. **Home Activity:*** Take turns picking one of these consonant blends and naming a word that begins or ends with that blend.

Name ______________________

Telephone Directory

A **telephone directory** lists phone numbers and addresses for people and businesses. The **white pages** list people and businesses in alphabetical order. The **yellow pages** contain advertisements and businesses, organized by category.

Directions: Read the following information from the yellow pages of a telephone directory. Then answer the questions below.

Party Supplies

BALLOONS AND COSTUMES
6080 Falls Rd. 555-9807

CLOWNING AROUND
12 Pine St. 555-6236

FUN FACTORY
1 Old Court Road 555-1428

GARRISON SHOPPING CENTER
34 Garrison Road 555-1928

LEAVE IT TO US: PARTY PLANNERS
718 6th Ave. 555-3335

PAPER PLUS OUTLET
The Store with Fun Stuff!
- Greeting Cards
- Balloons
- Gift Wrap
- Invitations

And More!
Mon.–Fri.: 10–9 Sat. 12–5
265 Mill Run Circle 555-0987

1. What category is used to organize these businesses? ABC order

2. If your class needed costumes, which business would you call? Explain.
I would call Balloons and Costumes because it has the word costumes in it,

3. Which business uses an advertisement? What information does an advertisement give that the other listings do not give?
____

4. Where would you find a listing for *Peter's Party Ideas?* Paper plus Outlet
____

5. If you had to call a new friend, would you look in the yellow pages or the white pages to find your friend's phone number? Explain.
White pages because it has phone numbers and adresses.

© Scott Foresman 3

Notes for Home: Your child answered questions about a telephone directory. ***Home Activity:*** Look through a local telephone directory. Challenge your child to find addresses and phone numbers of friends and local businesses.

Name ____________________

Cause and Effect

- A **cause** is why something happens. An **effect** is what happens.
- Sometimes an author uses clue words, such as *so* and *because,* to tell what happens and why.
- When there are no clue words, look for what happens and think about why it happens.

Cause → Effect

Directions: Reread "Fire!" Then complete the table. Explain what happens as a result of each story event.

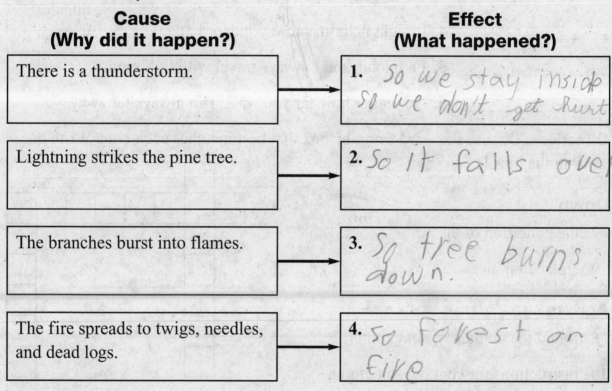

Cause (Why did it happen?)	Effect (What happened?)
There is a thunderstorm.	**1.** So we stay insid so we don't get hurt
Lightning strikes the pine tree.	**2.** So it falls over
The branches burst into flames.	**3.** So tree burns down.
The fire spreads to twigs, needles, and dead logs.	**4.** So forest on fire

5. Tell what effects a forest fire might have on the animals living there and people who hike and camp there. ____________________

____

____

© Scott Foresman 3

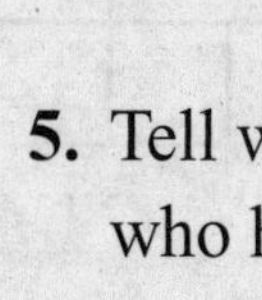

Notes for Home: Your child read a story and explained the effect of important events. ***Home Activity:*** Have your child describe something that has happened recently to him or her. Help your child identify what caused the event and what happened as a result.

Vocabulary

Directions: Choose the word from the box that best answers each riddle. Write the word on the line.

Check the Words You Know
__ distance
__ lightning
__ measured
__ recipe
__ thunder
__ weather

______________ **1.** Follow me carefully, and I'll give you something good to eat.

______________ **2.** I brighten the sky, and I always travel with thunder.

______________ **3.** The teaspoon did it. The tablespoon did it. The cup did it too!

______________ **4.** I might be rain, snow, wind, or hail.

______________ **5.** I am loud, and I always travel with lightning.

______________ **6.** No matter how far you walk, I'm always far away.

Directions: Choose the word from the box that best matches each clue. Write the word in the puzzle.

Down

7. the condition of the air

9. a place far away

Across

8. found the amount of something

10. instructions for cooking something

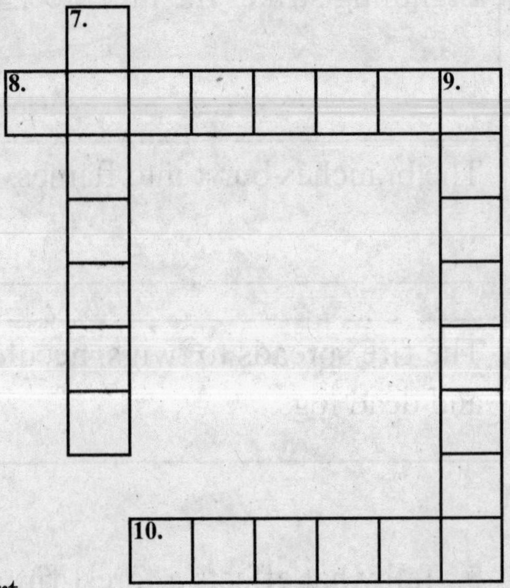

Write a Weather Report

On a separate sheet of paper, write a weather report. Try to predict what the weather will be like for the next few days using as many vocabulary words as possible.

© Scott Foresman 3

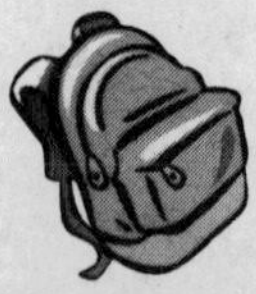

Notes for Home: Your child identified and used vocabulary words from *Thunder Cake*. ***Home Activity:*** Invite your child to be a TV weather announcer. Find or draw a map together. Ask your child to use the vocabulary words to predict weather for areas on the map.

Name ________________________

Cause and Effect

- A **cause** is why something happens. An **effect** is what happens.
- Sometimes an author uses clue words, such as *so* and *because,* to tell what happens and why. When there are no clue words, look for what happens and think about why it happens.

Directions: Reread what happens in *Thunder Cake* when the storm begins. Then answer the questions below.

The air was hot, heavy and damp. A loud clap of thunder shook the house, rattled the windows and made me grab her close.

"Steady, child," she cooed. "Unless you let go of me, we won't be able to make a Thunder Cake today!"

"Thunder Cake?" I stammered as I hugged her closer.

"Don't pay attention to that old thunder, except to see how close the storm is getting. When you see the lightning, start counting... real slow. When you hear the thunder, stop counting. That number is how many miles away the storm is. Understand?" she asked. "We need to know how far away the storm is, so we have time to make the cake and get it into the oven before the storm comes, or it won't be real Thunder Cake."

From THUNDER CAKE by Patricia Polacco. Copyright © 1990 by Babushka, Inc. Used by permission of Philomel Books, a division of Penguin Putnam Inc.

1. Why does the house shake and the windows rattle? The house shakes and the windows rattle because the storm is hear.

2. What makes the little girl grab her grandmother close? The storm makes her grab on to her grandma

3. Why do they need to know how far away the storm is? They have to know because they have to make thunder cake.

4. What clue word in the last sentence tells why something happens? so

5. Describe a cause-effect relationship in another part of the story. Write your description on another sheet of paper.

© Scott Foresman 3

Notes for Home: Your child identified causes and effects in a story. ***Home Activity:*** Take turns using the word *because* to describe some cause-effect relationships, such as *I skinned my knee because I fell down.*

Test-Taking Tips

1. Write your name on the test.
2. Read the directions carefully. Make sure you know exactly what you are supposed to do.
3. Read the question twice. Make sure you understand what the question is asking.
4. Read the answer choices for the question. Eliminate choices that do not make sense.
5. Mark your answer carefully.
6. Check your answer. Make sure that it makes the most sense out of all the answer choices.
7. If you have difficulty answering a question, you may want to go on to the next question. You can come back to difficult questions later.
8. If you finish the test early, go back and check all your answers.

© Scott Foresman 3

Selection Test

Directions: Choose the best answer to each item. Mark the space for the answer you have chosen.

Part 1: Vocabulary

Find the answer choice that means about the same as the underlined word in each sentence.

1. Dylan checked the weather.
   - plans for the day
   - time
   - what the air is like outside
   - news of the day

2. Thunder shook the house.
   - strong wind
   - land that moves
   - large tree
   - loud noise from a storm

3. Did you see the lightning?
   - rising sun
   - flash of electricity in the sky
   - kind of insect
   - dark cloud

4. We saw smoke in the distance.
   - place far away
   - house
   - low area of land
   - neighborhood

5. Sue measured a cup of milk.
   - drank
   - bought at the store
   - replaced
   - poured the right amount

6. What does the recipe say?
   - type of song
   - person who cooks
   - list of roads to take
   - set of directions for cooking

Part 2: Comprehension

Use what you know about the story to answer each item.

7. When the child first hears thunder, she—
   - hides under the bed.
   - begins to cry.
   - suggests baking a cake.
   - goes to gather eggs.

8. When does this story take place?
   - winter
   - spring
   - summer
   - fall

GO ON

© Scott Foresman 3

Name Matt Benson

9. The child counts between the lightning and thunder to find out—
   - what kind of storm is coming.
   - how far away the storm is.
   - how big a storm is coming.
   - where the storm is going.

10. What causes the windows to rattle?
   - the child's footsteps
   - a big farm truck that drives by
   - a flash of lightning
   - thunder

11. When the storm is right over them, the child and Babushka are—
   - gathering ingredients.
   - reading a story.
   - leaving the house.
   - frosting the cake.

12. What effect does Babushka's voice have on the child?
   - It calms her.
   - It scares her.
   - It angers her.
   - It excites her.

13. The most important change in the child happens when she—
   - overcomes her fear of storms.
   - learns to bake a cake.
   - learns to milk the cow.
   - takes eggs from the chickens.

14. From this story, you can tell that Babushka—
   - does not like to cook.
   - is afraid of lightning.
   - does not like the child.
   - has baked many times before.

15. The next time the child hears thunder, she will probably—
   - collect eggs and milk.
   - hide under the bed.
   - think of her grandmother.
   - write a story.

STOP

© Scott Foresman 3

Theme

REVIEW

Directions: Read each story. Then read each question about the story. Choose the best answer to the question. Mark the space for the answer you have chosen.

The Storm

A streak of lightning shot through the sky. Brian knew the storm would be coming soon. There was a lot of work to do before the rain started. Quickly, he led the cows into the barn and shut them in their stalls.

Brian's mom was riding the tractor. She had worked all morning but left the fields because of the storm.

Brian set out towards the horses. He led them back to their stalls. With a loud crash, thunder boomed in the sky. The horses were scared, so he gave them some oats and water.

Then Brian ran to the pig pen. He chased the pigs into their shelter. Lily was in the coop feeding the chickens.

Then the rain started. Large drops of water fell from the sky. Brian, Lily, and their mom ran towards their home. Wet and tired, the family had prepared the farm for the storm.

1. What is the theme of the story?
- It's fun on a farm.
- It rains on farms.
- Farms are a lot of work.
- Only children work on farms.

2. Which of these details supports the theme?
- Pigs squeal.
- Brian fed the horses.
- Brian likes horses.
- The rain started.

3. Which of these details supports the theme?
- Brian led the cows to their stalls.
- Brian ran into the house.
- Horses eat oats.
- They had horses.

4. Which of these details does **not** support the theme?
- Mom worked all morning.
- Lily fed the chickens.
- Brian fed the horses.
- The thunder was loud.

5. Which of these details does **not** support the theme?
- Big raindrops fell.
- Lily worked in the coop.
- Brian worked in the pig pen.
- Mom worked on the tractor.

© Scott Foresman 3

Notes for Home: Your child has identified the theme, or the big idea of a story. ***Home Activity:*** Take turns telling each other stories. Ask your child to identify the theme in each of the stories. Look for big ideas such as: *Honesty is the best policy.*

Name ______________________________________

Phonics: Diphthongs *oi* and *oy*

Directions: Read each sentence. Find and underline each word that has the same vowel sound you hear in **joy** and **spoil**. Write each word you underlined on the line.

______________ **1.** Ms. Chen heard the noise of the storm coming.

______________ **2.** She warned the boys to come in from the garden.

______________ **3.** Inside, they played with many different toys.

______________ **4.** They also sang songs. Their voices blended well.

______________ **5.** After the storm, they went back to digging up the soil in the garden.

______________ **6.** Ms. Chen went out to join them.

Directions: Say the name of each picture. Write **oi** or **oy** to complete each word.

7. c ___ ___ n

8. b ___ ___

9. ___ ___ l

10. t ___ ___ s

11. p ___ ___ nt

12. ___ ___ ster

13. b ___ ___ l

14. r ___ ___ alty

15. j ___ ___ n

© Scott Foresman 3

Notes for Home: Your child reviewed words with the vowels *oi* and *oy*. ***Home Activity:*** Give clues for each *oi* and *oy* word on this page and ask your child to guess the word. For example, *This can be a penny, a nickel, a dime, or a quarter. What is it? (a coin)*

Name ____________________

Phonics: Three-Letter Blends

REVIEW

Directions: Read each sentence. Say the underlined word in each sentence. Choose the word that has the same initial blend sound. Mark the space for the answer you have chosen.

1. Tim likes to eat strawberries.
- spring
- stars
- street
- stork

2. Millie has three dogs.
- thumbs
- thread
- tree
- thirteen

3. Spread the blanket on the grass.
- spoon
- stripe
- stool
- spring

4. The baby splashed the bath water.
- swam
- spy
- spray
- split

5. Ted scrubbed his desk clean.
- scrape
- scared
- skunk
- washed

6. Amanda squeezed the towel dry.
- skirt
- screen
- swan
- squid

7. Pam tied the gift with string.
- step
- rope
- strap
- stew

8. Wipe the dust off the TV screen.
- skip
- scream
- sore
- green

9. Look at the tiny sprout growing.
- sport
- seed
- street
- sprinkle

10. Kris threw the ball to Kat.
- then
- brew
- thimble
- thrill

© Scott Foresman 3

Notes for Home: Your child reviewed words that begin with the three-letter blends *str, thr, spr, spl, scr,* and *squ.* ***Home Activity:*** Say a word with one of these three-letter blends. Challenge your child to think of other words that begin with the same blend.

Name ______________________________________

Following Directions

When **following directions,** read all the directions first. Do each step one at a time. Follow directions in the order in which they are written.

Directions: Read the directions for figuring out how many miles lightning is from where you are. Then answer the questions.

- Watch for lightning to strike.
- When you see the lightning, start counting.
- When you hear the thunder, stop counting.
- Write the measurement "miles" after the number you counted to figure out how many miles the lightning is from where you are.
- Remember, always stay inside during a thunderstorm and keep a safe distance from windows.

1. Suppose you counted to 5 before you heard the thunder. How far away would the lightning be from where you are?

____

2. If the lightning were 7 miles away from you, how many numbers would you expect to count after seeing the lightning and before hearing the thunder?

____

3. Underline the second step you do to figure out the distance between the lightning and you.

4. Where is it safest to watch for lightning—indoors or outdoors? Explain.

____

____

5. Why is it important to follow directions in the order that they are written?

____

Notes for Home: Your child read a set of directions and answered questions about these directions. ***Home Activity:*** Write down simple directions for your child to follow. You might write directions telling your child how to set the table, use the washer or dryer, or wash the dishes.

© Scott Foresman 3

Name ______________________________

Compare and Contrast

- You **compare** when you say how things are alike.
- You **contrast** when you say how things are different.
- Clue words, such as *yet* and *however,* can signal a comparison or a contrast.

Directions: Reread "Afraid of the Dark!" Then complete the table. Tell how Osa acted at night. Then write a sentence that contrasts how Osa acts during the day and night.

Day	Night
Osa was lively.	**1.**
Osa climbed trees.	**2.**
She explored the valley.	**3.**
She was curious and collected things.	**4.**

5. Write a sentence that contrasts Osa in the day and Osa at night. Use a clue word such as *yet* or *however* in your sentence. ______________________________

____

____

© Scott Foresman 3

Notes for Home: Your child read a story and compared and contrasted a little girl's behavior in two different situations. ***Home Activity:*** Have your child compare and contrast two people in your family. Encourage your child to think about how each person looks and acts.

Name ______________________

Vocabulary

Directions: Cross out the word that does **not** belong in each group.

1. double	~~less~~	twice
2. seed	grain	~~juice~~
3. palace	~~yard~~	castle
4. reward	~~punishment~~	prize
5. single	one	~~two~~
6. thief	~~friend~~	robber

Check the Words You Know

- __ double
- __ grain
- √ palace
- √ reward
- √ single
- √ thief

Directions: Write a sentence for each vocabulary word below.

7. thief A theif stole a jewel in my house.

8. reward I got a reward for baseball.

9. single I only got a single grain of rice

10. palace I wish I owned a palace

Write a News Report

The king's castle has been robbed! On a separate piece of paper, write the news flash that a reporter would give about the crime. Use as many as vocabulary words as you can.

Notes for Home: Your child identified and used vocabulary words from *One Grain of Rice*. ***Home Activity:*** With your child, make up a fairy tale that takes place in a castle. Use as many vocabulary words as possible. Work together to illustrate the story.

© Scott Foresman 3

Name ______________________________

Compare and Contrast

- You **compare** when you say how things are alike.
- You **contrast** when you say how things are different.

Directions: Reread the two passages from *One Grain of Rice.* Then answer the questions below.

Passage 1

The raja's ministers implored him, "Your Highness, let us open the royal storehouses and give the rice to the people, as you promised."

"No!" cried the raja. "How do I know how long the famine may last? I must have the rice for myself. Promise or no promise, a raja must not go hungry!"

Passage 2

"And what will you do with this rice," said the raja with a sigh, "now that I have none?"

"I shall give it to all the hungry people," said Rani. "And I shall leave a basket of rice for you, too, if you promise from now on to take only as much rice as you need."

"I promise," said the raja.

From ONE GRAIN OF RICE: A MATHEMATICAL FOLKTALE by Demi. Published by Scholastic Press, a division of Scholastic Inc. Copyright © 1997 by Demi. Reprinted by permission of Scholastic Inc.

1. What words would you use to describe the raja's behavior in the first passage?
I think he is rude that he won't let them have the rice.

2. What words would you use to describe Rani's actions in the second passage?
I think fair that she let's the villadgers have most of the rice.

3. Write a sentence that compares or contrasts the raja and Rani. Raja is rude and Rani is fair.

4. Contrast the raja's behavior in the first passage with his behavior later.
In the first passadge he's greldy in the second he is nicer.

5. On a separate sheet of paper, contrast how the villagers' lives are at the beginning of the story and how they will be now.

© Scott Foresman 3

Notes for Home: Your child compared and contrasted characters in a story. ***Home Activity:*** Find pictures of two different people in a storybook or catalog. Have your child look at the pictures and tell how the people are alike and how they are different.

Name ______________________________

Test-Taking Tips

1. Write your name on the test.
2. Read the directions carefully. Make sure you know exactly what you are supposed to do.
3. Read the question twice. Make sure you understand what the question is asking.
4. Read the answer choices for the question. Eliminate choices that do not make sense.
5. Mark your answer carefully.
6. Check your answer. Make sure that it makes the most sense out of all the answer choices.
7. If you have difficulty answering a question, you may want to go on to the next question. You can come back to difficult questions later.
8. If you finish the test early, go back and check all your answers.

© Scott Foresman 3

Name ___________________________

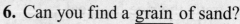

Selection Test

Directions: Choose the best answer to each item. Mark the space for the answer you have chosen.

Part 1: Vocabulary

Find the answer choice that means about the same as the underlined word in each sentence.

1. Lin gave me double the money.
   - twice as much
   - half of
   - some of
   - less than

2. I kept this single coin.
   - gold
   - one
   - new
   - large

3. Dad saw the thief leave.
   - person who steals
   - person who works
   - person who fights
   - person who yells

4. They gave him a reward.
   - call or request
   - piece of paper
   - long, written letter
   - prize for something done well

5. Would you like to live in a palace?
   - large tent
   - place for storing food
   - grand house of a ruler
   - secret place

6. Can you find a grain of sand?
   - pile
   - one very small piece
   - color
   - picture

Part 2: Comprehension

Use what you know about the story to answer each item.

7. Where does this story take place?
   - on a mountain
   - in China
   - on a farm
   - in India

8. The raja told the people he would store their rice until—
   - they needed it.
   - he sold it.
   - he and his court ate it.
   - his helpers gave it away.

GO ON

© Scott Foresman 3

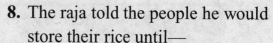

9. What happened before the famine?
- The raja held a feast.
- The raja went hungry.
- People had no rice to eat.
- Collectors took the people's rice.

10. When the famine came, the raja decided to—
- keep the rice for himself.
- trade the rice for meat.
- sell the rice to the people.
- give rice to the people.

11. Rani gathered the falling rice and returned it because she—
- was in love with the raja.
- planned to trick the raja.
- feared what the raja would do.
- had to keep the street clean.

12. When Rani made her deal with the raja, he thought she was—
- foolish.
- pretty.
- dishonest.
- shy.

13. Unlike the raja, Rani got her rice by—
- stealing.
- working hard.
- breaking promises.
- being clever.

14. Compared to before he met Rani, afterward the raja was—
- richer.
- better fed.
- wiser and fairer.
- more selfish.

15. When Rani gave out the rice, the people probably felt that—
- Rani was a rich person.
- the raja was a great man.
- the raja should leave the country.
- Rani had done a great thing.

STOP

© Scott Foresman 3

Name ______________________________

Predicting

REVIEW

Directions: Read the story. Then read each question about the story. Choose the best answer to the question. Mark the space for the answer you have chosen.

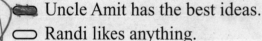

The Surprise

The whole Najir family was waiting for Uncle Amit. He had promised a surprise.

"Eat, Randi," her mother said, pushing the plate of rice toward her. However, Randi was too excited to eat.

Uncle Amit always had the best ideas. He had taken them camping overnight and boating on the harbor. Once, they spent the day at a rice factory. He would always tell them what to bring, but never where they were going.

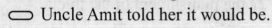

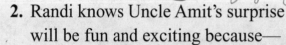

This time, Uncle Amit had told them to bring bathing suits and towels. Randi knew they must be going to the beach, but there had to be more to the surprise than that.

1. Which of these activities is **not** something Uncle Amit thought of to surprise the family?
   - boating on the harbor
   - camping overnight
   - an afternoon at a theater
   - a day at a rice factory

2. Randi knows Uncle Amit's surprise will be fun and exciting because—
   - Uncle Amit told her it would be.
   - Uncle Amit has the best ideas.
   - Randi likes anything.
   - her mom told her it would be.

3. Uncle Amit's plan will probably include—
   - sitting around a lot.
   - cold weather.
   - something boring.
   - something active and fun.

4. Which of these might be Uncle Amit's surprise?
   - playing board games
   - learning to clean the kitchen
   - watching TV
   - learning to water-ski

5. Which of these predictions seem likely based on what you already know?
   - Randi will have fun.
   - Uncle Amit won't show up.
   - Randi will stay home.
   - Uncle Amit won't have anything special planned.

© Scott Foresman 3

Notes for Home: Your child has used information in a story to make predictions about what might happen next. ***Home Activity:*** Read part of a story to your child. Then ask him or her what might happen next. Finish the story to see if your child's predictions were accurate.

Name Matt Benson

Word Study: Possessives

Directions: Draw a line from the words to the correct possessive form.

1. the doors of the palace

2. the punishment of the thief

3. the reward of the raja

4. the contents of the bags

5. the father of the princes

the palace's doors

the palaces' doors

the thief's punishment

the thieves' punishment

the rajas' reward

the raja's reward

the bags' contents

the bag's contents

the prince's father

the princes' father

Directions: Choose the word in ( ) that best completes each sentence. Write the word on the line.

mother's **6.** Stuart put some peas into his (mother's/mothers') bowl.

peas' **7.** The (peas'/pea's) bright green color made them look tasty.

guests' **8.** Many of the (guest's/guests') faces showed how hungry they were.

Stuart **9.** They wanted to taste the peas from (Stuarts'/Stuart's) garden too.

friend **10.** So Stuart filled all of his (friends'/friend's) plates high.

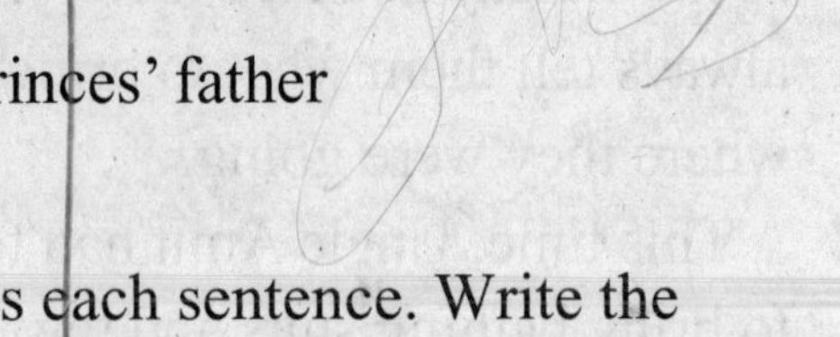

© Scott Foresman 3

Notes for Home: Your child reviewed words with singular and plural possessives. ***Home Activity:*** Ask your child to identify household items using singular or plural possessives. (For example: *This is Jack's bed,* or *These are my sisters' rooms.*)

Phonics: Diphthongs *oi* and *oy*

REVIEW

Directions: Read each sentence. Say the underlined word in each sentence. Choose the word that has the same vowel sound as in **oil** and **boy.** Mark the space for the answer you have chosen.

1. Tillie's favorite toy is her doll.
- doll
- treat
- loyal
- tie

2. Did Bess join the tennis team?
- joy
- job
- giant
- Jane

3. Hal always wears his cowboy hat.
- count
- bow
- boil
- bought

4. A voyage means the same as a trip.
- journey
- oyster
- violin
- cage

5. Nell found two coins on the street.
- cans
- money
- clown
- choice

6. Liz was annoyed with her sister.
- join
- angry
- any
- story

7. Plant the seeds deep in the soil.
- still
- sun
- dirt
- spoil

8. She has a beautiful singing voice.
- mice
- foil
- towel
- vacation

9. Jenna enjoyed the movie.
- liked
- entered
- destroy
- jeep

10. The horn made a big noise.
- nose
- point
- sound
- noose

© Scott Foresman 3

Notes for Home: Your child chose words that have the vowel sound heard in *oil* and *boy* spelled *oi* and *oy*. ***Home Activity:*** Help your child write words that rhyme with *oil* and *boy*.

Name ______________________

Bar Graphs/Circle Graphs

Graphs help you compare information easily. **Bar graphs** use horizontal or vertical bars to show information. **Circle graphs** have a pie shape and show information in each section.

Directions: The following bar graph and circle graph show data about a school fair about India. Decide which graph will help you answer each question. Then answer each question. Tell which graph you used.

Time Spent Preparing for the India Fair

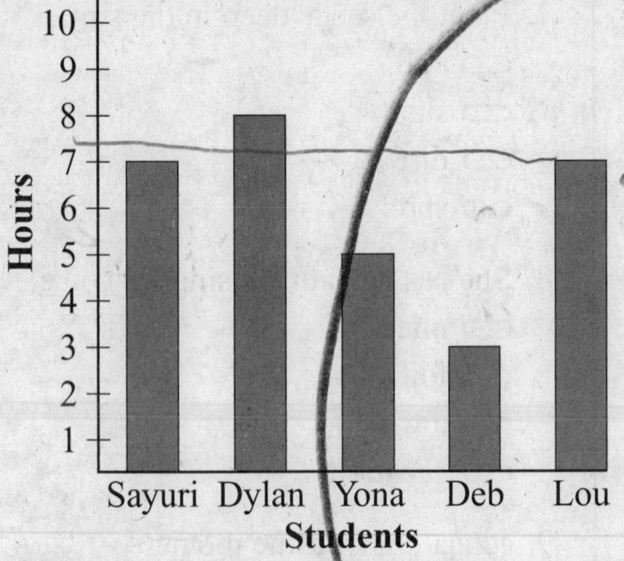

Number of Children Working at Fair Booths

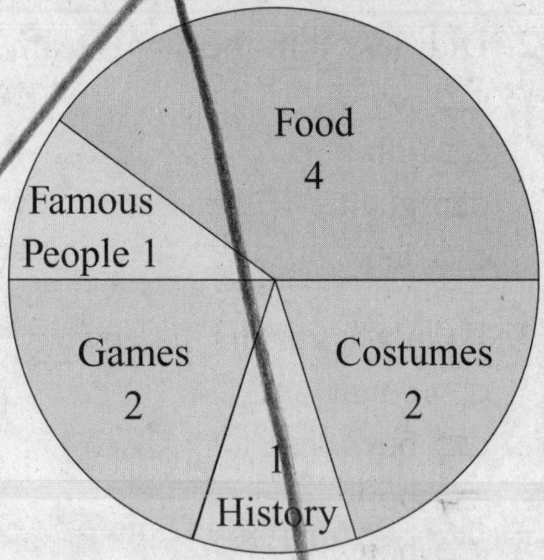

1. Who spent the most time preparing for the India fair? Dylan bar graph
2. How many hours did Lou spend preparing for the fair? 7½ bar graph
3. How many children worked at the food booth? 4 circle graph
4. Did more children work at the games booth or the history booth? Explain how you know.

More people worked at the games booth because two is more than one.

5. How many different kinds of booths were there at the fair? 5

Notes for Home: Your child answered questions by interpreting data in a bar graph and a circle graph. ***Home Activity:*** Together, record data about activities of family members, such as time spent brushing teeth. Help your child make a bar or circle graph to show the data.

© Scott Foresman 3

Name Matt

#1

Predicting

- To **predict** means to tell what you think might happen next in a story based on what has already happened.
- As you read, use the clues in a story and what you know from real life to help you decide what might happen next.

Directions: Reread "What to Do with an Old Hat." Then complete the table.

Questions	Explanations
What is the title of the story?	1. The title of the story is What to do with an Old Hat.
What can you predict about the story from its title?	2. I would predict that someone wants to get rit of an old hat.
What did you predict Uncle Nacho would do with his old hat?	3. I predicted that Uncle Nacho would throw the hat away.
What does Uncle Nacho finally do with his old hat?	4. Uncle Nacho finally threw the hat away
How close was your prediction to what actually happened?	5. My prediction was exactly right.

© Scott Foresman 3

Notes for Home: Your child made predictions about what will happen next in a story. ***Home Activity:*** Read the first half of a story to your child. Ask him or her to make predictions about what might happen next. Finish the story. Check your child's predictions.

Name ______________________________

Vocabulary

Directions: Choose the word from the box that best completes each sentence. Write the word on the line to the left.

Check the Words You Know
✓ arrived
✓ astonished
✓ cruel
✓ excitement
✓ respect
__ shone
__ spied
__ thirst

spied **1.** Joanne peeked through the window and _____ on the street merchants.

astonished **2.** She was surprised and _____ to see a woman yelling at the old man selling fish.

respect **3.** Joanne would never yell at someone that way because her mother had taught her to treat people with _____.

arrived **4.** When the doorbell rang she knew her friend Allison had _____.

cruel **5.** Joanne told Allison about the _____ woman yelling loudly at the man.

excitment **6.** Joanne's mother heard the _____ and went outside to check on the noise.

Directions: Draw a line to match each word with its definition.

7. shone	secretly watched
8. respect	gave off light
9. spied	a dry feeling in the mouth
10. thirst	show care for other people's feelings

Write a Newspaper Article

On a separate sheet of paper, write a newspaper article describing a local celebration or activity. Use as many vocabulary words as possible.

Notes for Home: Your child identified and used vocabulary words from *The Woman Who Outshone the Sun. **Home Activity:*** Read a story with your child. Ask him or her to use the words that surround an unknown word to figure out the meaning of unfamiliar words.

© Scott Foresman 3

Name ____________________

Draft

Predicting

- To **predict** means to tell what you think might happen next in a story based on what has already happened.
- As you read, use the clues in a story and what you know from real life to help you decide what might happen next.

Directions: Reread the part of *The Woman Who Outshone the Sun* where Lucia Zenteno leaves the village. Then answer the questions below.

> Everyone saw that Lucia Zenteno was leaving and that the river, the fishes, and the otters were leaving with her. The people were filled with despair. They had never imagined that their beautiful river would ever leave them, no matter what they did.
>
> Reprinted with permission of the publisher, Children's Book Press, San Francisco, CA. Copyright © 1991 by Children's Book Press and Rosalma Zubizarreta.

1. What is a likely prediction you could make after reading this first passage?

The villadge people would forgive her.

2. What clues in the passage could you use to make a prediction?

A woman got kicked out of a villadge and the river gote with her.

3. What do you know about what happens to rivers that dry up that might help you make predictions about this story?

I do not know about any l rivers that dry up

4. What do you think will happen the next time a stranger comes to the village?

The villadgers would not treat that person cruely.

5. On a separate sheet of paper, tell some of the predictions you made as you read the story. Did you have to change some of your predictions? What story clues did you use to make your predictions?

© Scott Foresman 3

Notes for Home: Your child answered questions about how to make predictions. ***Home Activity:*** Show your child pictures of people involved in different activities. Ask your child to make predictions about what he or she thinks might happen next for each activity.

Name ______________________________

Test-Taking Tips

1. Write your name on the test.
2. Read the directions carefully. Make sure you know exactly what you are supposed to do.
3. Read the question twice. Make sure you understand what the question is asking.
4. Read the answer choices for the question. Eliminate choices that do not make sense.
5. Mark your answer carefully.
6. Check your answer. Make sure that it makes the most sense out of all the answer choices.
7. If you have difficulty answering a question, you may want to go on to the next question. You can come back to difficult questions later.
8. If you finish the test early, go back and check all your answers.

© Scott Foresman 3

Name ______________________________

Selection Test

Directions: Choose the best answer to each item. Mark the space for the answer you have chosen.

Part 1: Vocabulary

Find the answer choice that means about the same as the underlined word in each sentence.

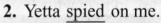

1. We arrived at two o'clock.
- came
- looked around
- left
- waited quietly

2. Yetta spied on me.
- made up names
- told stories
- kept secret watch
- tripped and fell

3. The cat's eyes shone.
- opened and closed
- were bright with light
- drew attention
- were dark

4. It was a cruel joke.
- very long
- planned to be fun
- causing pain
- silly

5. Fred was astonished.
- angry
- greatly surprised
- very happy
- uncomfortable

6. We could feel the excitement.
- fear; worry
- idea that something bad will happen
- sadness; grief
- feeling of being stirred up

7. Alice had a strong thirst.
- feeling of loneliness
- hunger for food
- need for attention
- dry feeling in the mouth

8. You should treat him with respect.
- honor
- sadness
- color
- sweets

© Scott Foresman 3

GO ON

Name ________________________________

Part 2: Comprehension

Use what you know about the story to answer each item.

9. When Lucia Zenteno came to the village, she walked with—
- a dog.
- a cat.
- an iguana.
- an otter.

10. The villagers were afraid of Lucia mainly because—
- the river loved her.
- she played tricks on them.
- she was beautiful.
- she was different.

11. The villagers drove Lucia away because—
- they were afraid of her.
- the river dried up.
- she took all the fish.
- her pet was dangerous.

12. Lucia asked the river to return after the villagers—
- held a feast in her honor.
- combed the fish from her hair.
- poured water over themselves.
- showed they were sorry.

13. Which words best describe Lucia?
- filled with shame
- mean and angry
- powerful but forgiving
- fun and popular

14. The next time a stranger comes to the village, the people will—
- ask the stranger to leave.
- treat the stranger kindly.
- call the stranger names.
- show their fear of strangers.

15. Which of these could happen in real life?
- The river fell in love with Lucia.
- Lucia combed her hair by the river.
- The fishes flowed out of her hair.
- The river left with Lucia.

STOP

© Scott Foresman 3

Name ____________________

Context Clues

REVIEW

Directions: Read the story. Then read each question about the story. Choose the best answer to the question. Mark the space for the answer you have chosen.

A Trip to the State Park

It was a very hot and sunny day. The children had packed water bottles to quench their thirst. They had to wear hats to protect themselves from the sun.

"Do you think we'll see any unusual plants?" asked Mr. Hernandez.

"I once saw a huge saguaro cactus growing in desert," replied Maria.

"Will we see any Gila monsters or other kinds of lizards?" asked Tom.

"We'll never know unless we get there!" said Tyrone. "Let's get on the bus."

When they had arrived at the State Park, they were greeted by their tour guide.

"Welcome!" she said. "Does each of you have a sombrero to cover your head? Okay, off we go to explore the park! I'll lead the group so I can show you things along the way."

1. What does the word quench mean?
- water bottle
- very hot
- to put an end to
- a very cold drink

2. What is a saguaro cactus?
- a kind of plant
- a kind of animal
- the name of the park
- a lizard

3. What is a Gila monster?
- a kind of plant
- a kind of lizard
- the name of the park
- an imaginary beast

4. What does a tour guide do?
- drives a bus
- welcomes new arrivals
- leads groups of people to show them new sights
- helps organize class trips to state parks

5. What is a sombrero?
- a ribbon
- a book
- an umbrella
- a hat

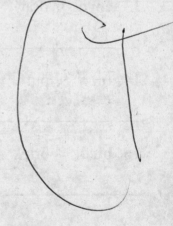

© Scott Foresman 3

Notes for Home: Your child has used context clues—words around unknown words—to figure out meanings in a story. ***Home Activity:*** As you read a story to your child, ask him or her to use context clues to figure the meaning of unfamiliar words.

Name ______________________________

Phonics: *r*-Controlled Vowels

Directions: Read the word at the top of each column. Choose two words from the box that have the same vowel sound spelled the same way. Write each word in the correct column.

flower	farm	skirt	turkey	storm	first	more	nurse	barn	tiger

park

1. farm
2. barn

her

3. flower
4. tiger

bird

5. skirt
6. first

for

7. more
8. storm

hurry

9. turkey
10. nurse

Directions: Circle the word that has the same vowel sound as the first word. Then write a sentence on the line that uses the word you circled.

11. far garden door red frog

The garden is beautiful

12. her cruel spring fern treat

I don't know what fern means.

13. corn draw fort rusty crew

I made a fort in my backyard

14. turn purse tan prize ripe

my mom has a purse.

15. bird brick dirt bead raise

There is a lot of dirt in my frontyard

© Scott Foresman 3

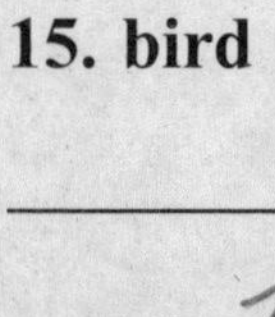

Notes for Home: Your child reviewed words with *r*-controlled vowel sounds, such as *far, her, corn, turn,* and *bird*. ***Home Activity:*** Ask your child to write a journal entry about a time he or she learned a lesson. Encourage your child to use words from this page.

Name ______________________________

REVIEW

Word Study: Suffixes *-ness*, *-ly*, *-ful*, *-ous*

Directions: Read each sentence. Choose the word that best completes the sentence. Mark the space for the answer you have chosen.

1. The star shone _____ in the sky.
- brightly
- happy
- brightness
- shining

2. Stu asked his sister's _____.
- forgiving
- forgiveness
- forgive
- forget

3. It was a beautiful and _____ day.
- gloomy
- glory
- glad
- glorious

4. My grandma is full of _____.
- lovely
- lovingly
- kindness
- kindly

5. I am filled with _____.
- happily
- happiness
- sad
- joyful

6. Having a new puppy is _____.
- wondering
- wonderful
- wonder
- winner

7. They ran _____ to the lake.
- quickly
- quick
- quickness
- slow

8. She has a _____ singing voice.
- beauty
- softness
- loudest
- beautiful

9. He tapped on the window _____.
- lightness
- lightly
- light
- softness

10. Drew's painting was _____.
- colorful
- coloring
- color
- colors

© Scott Foresman 3

Notes for Home: Your child completed sentences using words with the suffixes *-ness, -ly, -ful,* and *-ous*. ***Home Activity:*** Have your child think of additional words with these suffixes. Challenge him or her to use them in sentences.

Name ______________________________

Textbook/Trade Book

Textbooks teach about a particular subject matter, such as science, social studies, or math. **Trade books** are any books that are not textbooks, newspapers, magazines, or reference books, such as a dictionary.

Directions: Scan the following textbook page. Then answer the questions.

Chapter 5: ***MEXICO***

Lesson 1	The Land
Lesson 2	The People
Lesson 3	The History
Lesson 4	Mexico Today

Lesson 1 The Land

Physical Features Mexico has many different physical features. Its land is made up of plateaus (flat areas of land), mountains, coastal plains (flat areas of land near water), and peninsulas (areas of land nearly surrounded by water). The central Mexican Plateau makes up most of Mexico. There are mountains on the east, west, and south sides of the Mexican Plateau. There are coastal plains on the east and west sides. There are two major peninsulas: the Yucatan in the southeast and Baja California in the northwest.

Plant and Animal Life Plant and animal life vary depending on the climate. Cactus, agaves, and yucca grow in the dry areas. In the wetter areas, there are rainforests and savannas. Birds, reptiles, monkeys, jaguars, and tapirs live in the south. Armadillo, deer, pumas, and coyotes live in the north.

1. What is the title of Chapter 5? ______________________________

2. How many lessons are in this chapter? ______________________________

3. In which lesson would you look in to find out about the different groups of people living in Mexico?

____

4. Under which subheading in Lesson 1 can you find information about the different types of wildlife that live in Mexico?

____

5. Suppose you read a realistic story about a young boy who lives on a farm in Mexico. What could you learn about Mexico from reading this trade book?

____

____

Notes for Home: Your child answered questions about a textbook page and a trade book. ***Home Activity:*** Look through one of your child's textbooks with him or her. Have your child point out the different features. Ask your child to find specific kinds of information.

© Scott Foresman 3

Name ______________________________

Making Judgments

- A **judgment** is your opinion about a character, a situation, an action, or an idea in a story or article.
- When you **make judgments,** you use what you already know and what you read.
- Find sentences from the story or article to support your judgment.

Directions: Reread "Grandpa's Memories." Then complete the table. Write a judgment for each event telling whether you think something is good or bad, fair or unfair. Be sure to give a reason to support your judgment.

Event	Judgment
The boy sees a plane in the sky.	**1.** Bad because he'll want to see it land and stand it will take time off of the dads work.
Both boys have chores to do each day.	**2.** Good because it gets a lot done around the farm.
The boy promises to weed the garden if his dad takes him to see the plane.	**3.** Fair because the boy is doing an extra chore to see something.
The barnstormer charges money for an airplane ride.	**4.** Unfair because the boy doesn't have any money and it's his first time on a plane.
The boy dreams of flying next summer.	**5.** Good because it's his dream and it's his favorite thing.

© Scott Foresman 3

Notes for Home: Your child read a story and made judgments about the characters and their actions. ***Home Activity:*** Read a story with your child. Ask your child to judge specific actions by its characters. Have your child decide if these actions are good or bad, fair or unfair.

Name ______________________________

Vocabulary

Directions: Choose the word from the box that best completes each sentence. Write the word on the line to the left.

Check the Words You Know
- __ compasses
- __ engine
- __ flight
- __ instruments
- __ route
- __ soars

___flight___ **1.** Our guides were trying to find a _____ through the forest.

___compasses___ **2.** They were using their maps and _____.

___routes___ **3.** I wished they had even more _____ that could help us find our way.

___engine___ **4.** We knew we were near the highway when we heard the sound of a truck's _____.

Directions: Choose the word from the box that best matches each clue. Write the word in the puzzle.

Down

5. devices for measuring, recording, or controlling

7. a plan for going somewhere

8. a trip in an airplane

Across

6. tools for showing directions

9. the part of a machine that makes it move or run

10. flies at a great height

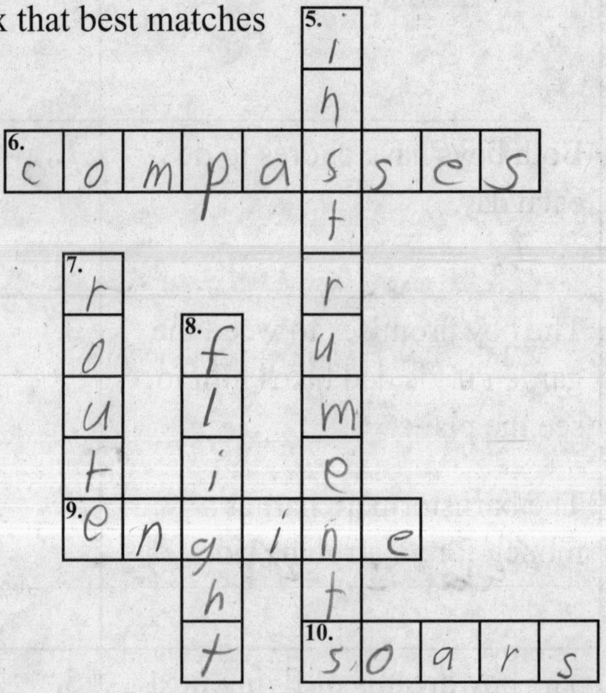

Write an Advertisement

Imagine you own an airline. On a separate sheet of paper, write an advertisement to tell people about your airline. Use as many vocabulary words as you can.

© Scott Foresman 3

Notes for Home: Your child identified and used vocabulary words from *Flight: The Journey of Charles Lindbergh*. ***Home Activity:*** Act out flying a plane as captain and co-pilot with your child. Talk to each other as if you are in the cockpit. Use the vocabulary words listed.

Name ______________________________

Making Judgments

- A **judgment** is your opinion about a character, a situation, an action, or an idea in a story or article.
- When you **make judgments,** you use what you already know and what you read. Find sentences from the story or article to support your judgment.

Directions: Reread what happens in *Flight: The Journey of Charles Lindbergh* when Lindbergh dozes for a moment. Then answer the questions below.

Space and time and deep, deep darkness . . . Lindbergh has been awake for almost fifty hours straight. He is closer to Europe than America. Now there is no turning back, only moving forward. He dozes for a minute and then jerks awake. One of the plane's wings is dipping crazily.

In a sudden rush of fear, he grabs for the throttle. He gropes for the steady center with his heart pounding. As he feels the leveling wings, he lets out breath. He repeats over and over to himself: *I must not sleep, I must not sleep.* Here, high above the churning ocean, to sleep is to die!

From FLIGHT: THE JOURNEY OF CHARLES LINDBERGH by Robert Burleigh. Copyright © 1991 by Robert Burleigh, text. Copyright © 1991 by Mike Wimmer, illustrations. Used by permission of Philomel Books, a division of Penguin Putnam Inc.

1. Why can't Lindbergh turn back? He can't turn back because he's closer to Eurepe than America.

2. Why is it so important for Lindbergh to stay awake? It is important because if he falls asleep he might crash.

3. Why does the plane almost crash? It almost crashes because the wing dipping crazily.

4. How does Lindbergh feel when he steadies the plane? How do you know?

____

5. Do you think Lindbergh's flight was worth all the dangers? Explain your judgment on a separate sheet of paper. Use examples from the story to support it.

Yes because if he didn't do it he wouldn't be famous.

Notes for Home: Your child read a story and used details from the story to make judgments. ***Home Activity:*** Work with your child to make up a story about a heroic character. Ask your child to decide how a hero should act.

© Scott Foresman 3

Name ______________________________

Test-Taking Tips

1. Write your name on the test.
2. Read the directions carefully. Make sure you know exactly what you are supposed to do.
3. Read the question twice. Make sure you understand what the question is asking.
4. Read the answer choices for the question. Eliminate choices that do not make sense.
5. Mark your answer carefully.
6. Check your answer. Make sure that it makes the most sense out of all the answer choices.
7. If you have difficulty answering a question, you may want to go on to the next question. You can come back to difficult questions later.
8. If you finish the test early, go back and check all your answers.

© Scott Foresman 3

Name ______________________________

Selection Test

Directions: Choose the best answer to each item. Mark the space for the answer you have chosen.

Part 1: Vocabulary

Find the answer choice that means about the same as the underlined word in each sentence.

1. We followed the route.
   - way to go
   - large truck
   - sign
   - directions

2. The hikers used their compasses.
   - water bottles
   - tools for setting up tents
   - fire starters
   - tools for showing direction

3. The large bird soars.
   - sings loudly
   - flies at a great height
   - swims fast
   - cleans its feathers

4. That is an old engine.
   - part of a machine that makes it run
   - large, soft chair
   - book of road maps
   - tool used to repair flat tires

5. You must clean the instruments.
   - special clothes for a certain job
   - bottles of medicine
   - things made of glass
   - tools for measuring or recording

6. The flight took three hours.
   - test
   - trip in an airplane
   - talk between two people
   - meal

Part 2: Comprehension

Use what you know about the selection to answer each item.

7. Lindbergh flew across the—
   - Pacific Ocean.
   - entire United States.
   - Atlantic Ocean.
   - South Pole.

8. Lindbergh left his radio behind in order to—
   - see straight ahead.
   - fly in a straight line.
   - make sure no one bothered him.
   - make his plane lighter.

© Scott Foresman 3

GO ON

9. Lindbergh wrote notes during his trip because he wanted to—
- keep himself awake.
- remember everything.
- prove he made the trip.
- be a writer instead of a pilot.

10. Lindbergh flew up very high at one point. Why did he have to go back down again?
- There was too much fog.
- Ice formed on the plane's wings.
- His compasses did not work.
- He needed to see the ocean so he could tell where he was.

11. Which sentence best describes Charles Lindbergh?
- He was easily frightened.
- He was not very intelligent.
- He did what he wanted to do.
- He was a sad, lonely person.

12. What was the hardest part of the flight for Lindbergh?
- taking off safely
- landing
- staying on course
- staying awake

13. Lindbergh decided not to eat during the flight because he—
- thought it was easier to stay awake on an empty stomach.
- thought he might get sick.
- didn't like the food he had.
- needed both hands to steer.

14. Which detail best shows how strong Lindbergh's dream was?
- He felt happy when he saw Paris.
- He saw many small lights just before landing.
- He decided to go all the way to Paris instead of landing in Ireland.
- Lindbergh answered many questions about his flight.

15. To Lindbergh, what was the worst thing that happened after he landed in Paris?
- Two French pilots helped him.
- People began to tear off pieces of his plane.
- He had to answer questions.
- People carried him on their shoulders.

STOP

© Scott Foresman 3

Name ______________________________

Text Structure

REVIEW

Directions: Read the story. Then read each question about the story. Choose the best answer to the question. Mark the space for the answer you have chosen.

A Young Boy's First Flight

Rick was scared. "This plane is so big," he said. "How can it ever fly?"

Rick's mom smiled. "Don't worry, Rick. Think about Grandma and how happy she will be to see you."

Rick's grandmother was sick. She had asked Rick and his mom to come for a visit. Rick had not wanted to get on the airplane, but he did want to help his grandmother get well.

The plane began to move. Rick held his mom's hand. She smiled. Rick felt a little better.

Suddenly the plane lifted off the ground. Rick watched the buildings and trees get smaller and smaller. It was fun to move so fast through the air and watch the world below. Rick turned to his mom and hugged her. "I can't wait to see Grandma!" he said.

1. This story tells about—
- ○ how to fly a plane.
- ○ a real-life famous pilot.
- ● made-up characters.
- ○ talking animals.

2. This story starts when Rick—
- ○ sees his grandmother.
- ● is on the plane.
- ○ arrives at the airport.
- ○ takes off in the plane.

3. Rick's grandmother gets sick—
- ○ before Rick gets on the plane.
- ● when Rick arrives at the airport.
- ○ while Rick is on the plane back.
- ○ after Rick and his mother go back home.

4. When the plane starts to move, Rick—
- ○ smiles.
- ○ asks how planes can fly.
- ● hugs his mom.
- ○ holds his mom's hand.

5. At the end of the story, Rick feels—
- ○ sick.
- ○ scared.
- ● excited.
- ○ sad.

© Scott Foresman 3

Notes for Home: Your child reviewed text structure—the way a piece of writing is organized. ***Home Activity:*** Read a story with your child and talk about how it is organized. Was the story about real people or made-up characters? Are events told in the order they happen?

Name ______

Word Study: Plurals

Directions: Use the plural form of each word in ( ) to complete each sentence. Write the word on the line.

feet **1.** John put his boots on his (foot).

shelves **2.** He took his things off the (shelf) and put them in his backpack.

compasses **3.** He grabbed one of the (compass) to help him find his way.

sentries **4.** John slipped outside and looked for the (sentry) guarding the border.

miles **5.** He had to walk many (mile) to find freedom.

stars **6.** He traveled at night with only the moon and (star) to light his way.

trees **7.** By daylight he hid among the (tree) and slept.

mouses **8.** On the third night, he found that (mouse) had eaten his food.

leaves **9.** He ate (leaf) and berries to stay alive.

days **10.** After eight long (day), he finally made it back to his homeland.

Directions: Write the plural form of each word below.

11. instrument instrument

12. roof rooves

13. woman women

14. engine engines

15. deer deers

16. tooth teeth

17. branch branches

18. knife knives

19. plane planes

20. pony ______

© Scott Foresman 3

Notes for Home: Your child reviewed plurals—words naming more than one person, place, or thing. ***Home Activity:*** Work with your child to make a list of people, places, and things from his or her favorite story. Ask your child to write the plural of each word.

Name ____________________________________

Word Study: Possessives

REVIEW

Directions: Read each sentence. Say the underlined word in each sentence. Choose the word that is the possessive form of the underlined word. Mark the space for the answer you have chosen.

1. Water covers most of Earth.
- ⬭ Earths
- ⬭ Earthes
- ⬭ Earth's
- ⬭ Earths's

2. Lindbergh was a famous pilot.
- ⬭ Lind's
- ⬭ Lindbergh's
- ⬭ Lindbergh'
- ⬭ Lindberghs

3. The airplane soared away.
- ⬭ airplanes'
- ⬭ airplanes
- ⬭ planes
- ⬭ airplane's

4. The plane landed at the airfield.
- ⬭ airfield's
- ⬭ airfields
- ⬭ airfields'
- ⬭ airfields's

5. Pilots use instruments.
- ⬭ instrument's
- ⬭ instruments'
- ⬭ instruments's
- ⬭ instrument

6. The engine made a lot of noise.
- ⬭ engine's
- ⬭ engines
- ⬭ engines'
- ⬭ engineer

7. Compasses show direction.
- ⬭ compass's
- ⬭ compasses
- ⬭ compasses'
- ⬭ compasses's

8. Women have been great pilots too.
- ⬭ woman
- ⬭ women's
- ⬭ womens's
- ⬭ woman's

9. My friends all like planes.
- ⬭ friends'
- ⬭ friends
- ⬭ friend's
- ⬭ friendly

10. Chris wrote a report on planes.
- ⬭ Chris's
- ⬭ Chrises
- ⬭ Chris'
- ⬭ Chris

© Scott Foresman 3

Notes for Home: Your child reviewed possessives of singular and plural nouns. ***Home Activity:*** Read an article together. Ask your child to point out possessives. Have him or her tell whether the possessive shows ownership by one or by more than one.

Name ______________________________

Technology: Atlas

An **atlas** is a book of maps. There are CD-ROM atlases that contain maps too. Since CD-ROMs can store a lot of information in a small amount of space, you can find maps of countries, states, cities, and even streets all on one slim CD-ROM.

Directions: Look at the map of Utah. Use the map to answer the questions.

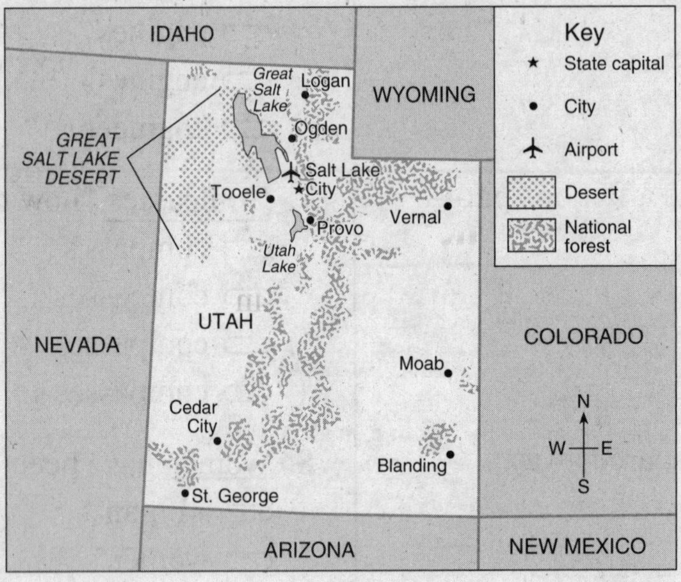

1. What is the capital of Utah? Salt Lake City
2. What are the names of two lakes in Utah? Great Salt Lake Utah
3. The airport is located near which city? Salt Lake City
4. In what direction would you travel if you flew a plane from Salt Lake City over the Great Salt Lake Desert?

   West
5. Why might school libraries want to have CD-ROM atlases instead of atlases printed in books?

   ____

   ____

Notes for Home: Your child used a map to answer questions. ***Home Activity:*** Find an atlas. Ask your child to select a map to study in detail. Look at the map together. Ask your child to name three things he or she learned from the map.

© Scott Foresman 3

Name ______________________

Fact and Opinion

- A **statement of fact** can be proved true or false.
- A **statement of opinion** is what someone believes or thinks and cannot be proved true or false.
- Words that express what someone feels or thinks, such as *believe, could, like,* and *good,* are clues to a statement of opinion.

Directions: Reread "Moving Along on Bike Trails." Then complete the table. Tell whether each statement is a statement of fact or opinion. Write an **X** in the correct column to show your answer.

Statement	Fact	Opinion
1. Kathy Felix and Michelle Bigger got stuck in traffic.	X	
2. Kathy and Michelle live in the Indian Oaks subdivision.	X	
3. Kathy and Michelle think more bike paths are needed.		X
4. Bike riding on busy roads is scary.		X
5. The new bike trail system would serve people who ride for recreation or for transportation.	X	
6. A survey showed more people in the community are interested in biking than any other recreation.	X	
7. A bike trail should be built along the DuPage River.		X
8. John Vann is the assistant director for parks and planning.	X	
9. Riding bikes is a good form of exercise.		X
10. More people should try riding bikes instead of driving cars.		X

© Scott Foresman 3

Notes for Home: Your child identified statements of fact and statements of opinion. ***Home Activity:*** Read a newspaper article with your child. Discuss with your child which statements are statements of fact and which are statements of opinion.

Name ____________________

Vocabulary

Directions: Choose the word from the box that best completes each sentence. Write the word on the line to the left.

Check the Words You Know
__ avenue
__ ducklings
__ nest
__ pool
__ splash
__ spring

avenue **1.** Jackie lives on a wide _____.

pool **2.** There is a small _____ of still water in her backyard.

spring **3.** When the weather turned warm in _____, two ducks came to visit.

_______________ **4.** Two ducks built a _____ near the water.

_______________ **5.** The ducks raised five _____ there.

_______________ **6.** The baby birds like to _____ in the water.

Directions: Choose the word from the box that best matches each picture. Write the word on the line.

_______________ **7.** 

_______________ **8.** 

_______________ **9.** 

_______________ **10.** 

Write a Letter

On a separate sheet of paper, write a letter to a friend about a trip to the park. Use as many vocabulary words as you can.

© Scott Foresman 3

Notes for Home: Your child identified and used vocabulary words from the story *Chibi: A True Story from Japan*. ***Home Activity:*** Invite your child to draw a picture for each vocabulary word. Help your child write captions under each picture to tell a story about ducklings.

Name Matt Benson

Fact and Opinion

- A **statement of fact** can be proved true or false.
- A **statement of opinion** is what someone believes or thinks and cannot be proved true or false.
- Words that express what someone feels or thinks, such as *believe, could, like,* and *good,* are clues to a statement of opinion.

Directions: Reread what happens in *Chibi: A True Story from Japan* when Oka-san takes her ducklings for a walk. Then answer the questions below.

One morning in June, Oka-san hastily quack-quacked the ducklings together. When they were all in a line, she marched them to one of the exits and right out of the office park! Sato-san and the other duck watchers trailed after her at a safe distance. When she reached the corner, Oka-san stopped short, turned, and waddled all the way back to the pool, her ducklings right behind her.

She repeated the trip seven times that morning.

"What is that crazy Oka-san doing?" people asked one another.

Excerpt from CHIBI: A TRUE STORY FROM JAPAN. Text copyright © 1996 by Barbara Brenner and Julia Takaya. Reprinted by permission of Clarion Books/Houghton Mifflin Company. All rights reserved.

1.–2. Write two statements of fact about the first paragraph.

1. It was a June morning.

2. Okosan-San called the ducklings toget

3. Was it a statement of fact or opinion when the duck watchers called Oka-san crazy? Explain.

It is an opinion because some people might not think shes crazy.

4. Was it a statement of fact or opinion that Oka-san repeated the trip seven times? Explain.

It is a fact because it really did happen.

5. Find other examples of statements of fact and opinion in the rest of the story. Explain why the statement is a fact or opinion.

© Scott Foresman 3

Notes for Home: Your child read a story and identified statements of fact and opinion. ***Home Activity:*** Read advertisements with your child. Discuss which statements are statements of fact and which are statements of opinion.

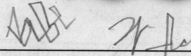

Name ____________________

Test-Taking Tips

1. Write your name on the test.
2. Read the directions carefully. Make sure you know exactly what you are supposed to do.
3. Read the question twice. Make sure you understand what the question is asking.
4. Read the answer choices for the question. Eliminate choices that do not make sense.
5. Mark your answer carefully.
6. Check your answer. Make sure that it makes the most sense out of all the answer choices.
7. If you have difficulty answering a question, you may want to go on to the next question. You can come back to difficult questions later.
8. If you finish the test early, go back and check all your answers.

© Scott Foresman 3

Selection Test

Directions: Choose the best answer to each item. Mark the space for the answer you have chosen.

Part 1: Vocabulary

Find the answer choice that means about the same as the underlined word in each sentence.

1. Sandy crossed the avenue.
- bridge
- railroad tracks
- wide street
- small stream

2. It was a warm spring day.
- season between winter and summer
- bright and sunny
- time of year when leaves fall
- rainy and wet

3. Jen fell into the pool.
- small body of still water
- flower garden
- empty lot in a city
- group of plants

4. Tina landed with a splash.
- wide smile on her face
- large bubble
- act of making water fly about
- loud noise

5. Brendan found a nest.
- place where birds lay eggs
- old tool made from stone
- special surprise
- picture book

6. The ducklings walked in a row.
- wild ducks
- mother ducks
- very old ducks
- young ducks

Part 2: Comprehension

Use what you know about the selection to answer each item.

7. Where does the mother duck land at the start of the story?
- in a small Japanese town
- on top of Mount Fuji
- in a pool outside an office building in Tokyo
- in the middle of a wide street

8. When people first heard about the duck family, they—
- asked the Emperor to help the ducks.
- came to visit the ducks.
- tried to take the ducks home.
- tried to take the ducks to a zoo.

GO ON

© Scott Foresman 3

Name Matt Benson

9. Who gave Chibi her name?
- ⬭ a child
- ⬭ an office worker
- ⬬ a news photographer
- ⬭ a food seller

10. People paid a lot of attention to Chibi because she was the—
- ⬭ prettiest.
- ⬭ oldest.
- ⬭ bravest.
- ⬬ smallest.

11. The ducks surprised everyone by—
- ⬭ sleeping through the night.
- ⬭ refusing to eat any food.
- ⬭ crossing the highway at night.
- ⬬ using a different exit than people expected.

12. As he tried to save the ducks, what did Sato-san do that was dangerous?
- ⬬ He ran into traffic.
- ⬭ He dropped his camera.
- ⬭ He climbed over some bushes.
- ⬭ He stayed up all night.

13. The author most likely used some Japanese words in this selection to—
- ⬭ confuse readers.
- ⬭ help readers learn Japanese.
- ⬭ surprise readers.
- ⬬ give a feeling of Japan.

14. Which sentence states a fact?
- ⬭ Oka-san was a crazy duck.
- ⬭ Across the street was a great place for ducklings.
- ⬬ Lights went on in the city.
- ⬭ The ducks were very exciting.

15. Which sentence gives an opinion?
- ⬭ The car stopped.
- ⬭ Sato-san took pictures.
- ⬭ The mother duck quacked.
- ⬬ Chibi was the cutest duck.

STOP

© Scott Foresman 3

Name ______________________________

Visualizing

REVIEW

Directions: Read the story. Then read each question about the story. Choose the best answer to the question. Mark the space for the answer you have chosen.

A Day at the Pond

Sunlight danced across the water. Becca took off her shoes and waded into the pond. Her feet sank into the soft, squishy mud.

Two ducks swam toward her very fast. Becca could hear the steady mumble of their quacking. She threw them a chunk of bread.

"Hey!" Becca yelled as the bigger duck pushed the smaller duck out of the way. "You're greedy." Every time Becca threw a piece of bread, the big duck grabbed it.

"Here," she said to the smaller duck. "This one is for you." She threw a piece of bread right to the little duck. Becca laughed as the little duck grabbed the bread in its beak and swallowed it. "I'm glad you like it," she said. "I'll come back tomorrow with more."

1. What kind of day is it?
   - cloudy
   - rainy
   - sunny
   - chilly

2. The mud feels—
   - hard and dry.
   - painful.
   - slimy.
   - soft and squishy.

3. Becca can hear—
   - ducks quacking.
   - insects humming.
   - birds singing.
   - wind blowing.

4. The ducks swim
   - very fast.
   - in a circle.
   - slowly.
   - with their heads under the water.

5. When she feeds the ducks, Becca is probably—
   - smiling.
   - frowning.
   - crying.
   - sneezing.

© Scott Foresman 3

Notes for Home: Your child reviewed visualizing story details. ***Home Activity:*** Work with your child to write a paragraph describing a place. Include details about the place's sights, sounds, smells, and tastes, as well as things you can touch there.

Name ______________________________

Phonics: Consonant /k/ Spelled *c, ck, ch*

Directions: Underline the letter or letters that stand for the sound /k/ in each word.

1. rock
2. ache
3. colored
4. corner
5. duck
6. music
7. caught
8. tracking
9. chorus
10. circle
11. stomach
12. traffic

Directions: Say the name of each picture. Write the missing letters to complete each word.

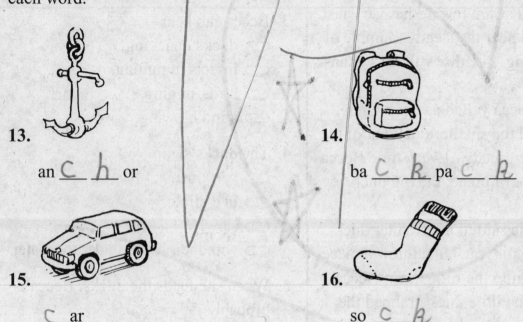

13. an c h or

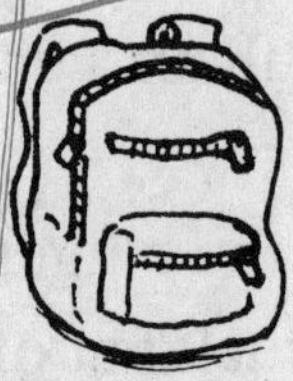

14. ba c k pa c k

15. c ar

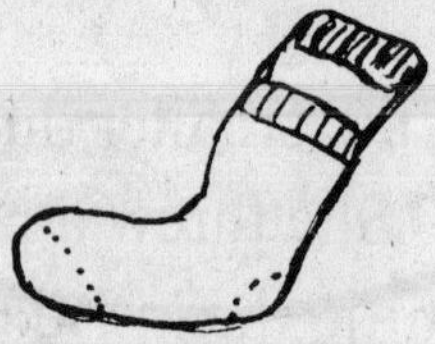

16. so c k

Directions: Choose the word that has the sound /k/ to complete each sentence. Write the word on the line.

backyard **17.** Kim and Ken heard a strange noise coming from their (cellar/backyard).

knocking **18.** It sounded like someone (knocking/dancing).

climbed **19.** Then Ken (searched/climbed) their small Japanese maple tree.

woodpecker **20.** "Look, Kim!" he called. "It's a (finch/woodpecker)!"

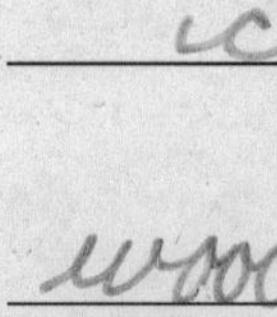

Notes for Home: Your child reviewed words with the sound /k/ as in *car, anchor,* and *duck.* ***Home Activity:*** Read a story with your child. Encourage your child to identify and say words containing the sound /k/. Together, make a list of these words.

© Scott Foresman 3

Name ____________________

Phonics: *r*-Controlled Vowels

REVIEW

Directions: Read each sentence. Say the underlined word in each sentence. Choose the word that has the same vowel sound as the underlined word. Mark the space for the answer you have chosen.

1. I get up early each <u>morning</u>.
- corn
- Monday
- money
- market

2. Wait <u>for</u> me!
- front
- fountain
- foam
- fork

3. I'd like <u>more</u> milk, please.
- chirp
- charge
- churn
- chore

4. I have <u>four</u> sisters.
- fort
- foal
- full
- phone

5. The wolf howled <u>mournfully</u>.
- mountain
- mouse
- morning
- mole

6. I went to see <u>her</u> last night.
- hear
- there
- heart
- learn

7. She did the work by <u>herself</u>.
- shirt
- short
- scrape
- shut

8. I brought soup in my <u>thermos</u>.
- third
- there
- theme
- the

9. The car <u>swerved</u> on the road.
- save
- curve
- sunny
- swing

10. I <u>heard</u> the dog bark.
- fern
- friend
- forth
- freckle

© Scott Foresman 3

Notes for Home: Your child reviewed words where the letter *r* changes the way a vowel sounds. ***Home Activity:*** Look through a story with your child to find words spelled with *or, ore, our, er, ear,* and *ir*. Make a list of these words and match words that have the same vowel sound.

Name ______________________________

Signs

Signs use pictures or symbols and sometimes words to communicate a message. Some signs may give information about upcoming events.

Directions: Look at each road sign. Match each sign with the correct message. Draw a line from the sign to the message.

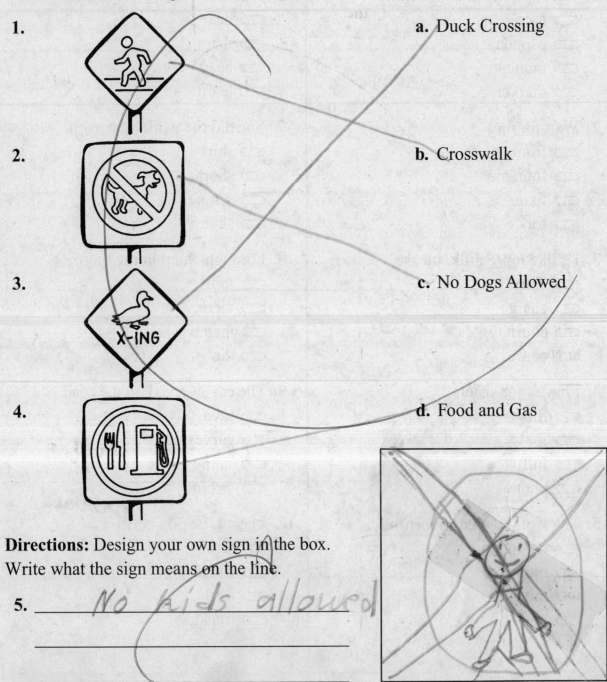

1. 

2. 

3. 

4. 

a. Duck Crossing

b. Crosswalk

c. No Dogs Allowed

d. Food and Gas

Directions: Design your own sign in the box. Write what the sign means on the line.

5. No kids allowed

Notes for Home: Your child identified the meaning of different signs and designed a sign. *Home Activity:* Go on a sign hunt in your home or in your neighborhood. Work together to find signs and figure out their meanings. Include flyers that describe neighborhood events.

© Scott Foresman 3

Predicting

- To **predict** means to tell what you think might happen next in a story based on what has already happened.
- A prediction is what you say will happen.
- As you read, use what you know from your own life and from what you've learned and look for clues in the story that help you decide what might happen next.

Directions: Reread "Keep the Buckets Coming." Think about what you predicted would happen once the volunteer fire department arrived. Then complete the table by answering questions about your prediction.

Question	Explanation
What did you predict would happen once the volunteer fire department arrived?	1. I predicted that they would easily get it out.
What story clues or life experiences did you use to make your prediction?	2. I used the picture in the backround and it wasn't that big.
How close was your prediction to what really happened?	3. My prediction was off by a lot.
What do you think the family will do now that the fire is out?	4. They will probably call somone to fix there house.
What might have happened if the volunteer fire department hadn't arrived?	5. They would probably be going for a long time.

© Scott Foresman 3

Notes for Home: Your child made a prediction and explained why he or she made that prediction. ***Home Activity:*** Read a story with your child. Pause often and ask him or her to predict what will happen next. Continue reading to check your child's predictions.

Name ____________________

Vocabulary

Directions: Draw a line to match each word with its definition.

1. howling	air in motion
2. snatched	a mournful or sad cry
3. stumble	grabbed suddenly
4. whirled	walk unsteadily
5. wind	moved suddenly

Check the Words You Know

__ howling
__ snatched
__ stumble
__ whipped
__ whirled
__ wind

Directions: Choose the word from the box that best replaces the underlined word or words. Write the word on the line.

______________ **6.** I quickly grabbed my raincoat and went out to see the storm.

______________ **7.** The wind moved quickly through the trees.

______________ **8.** It was making a long crying noise like a wolf!

______________ **9.** Leaves spun around in the air.

______________ **10.** The storm was so strong that it made me trip on my way back to the house.

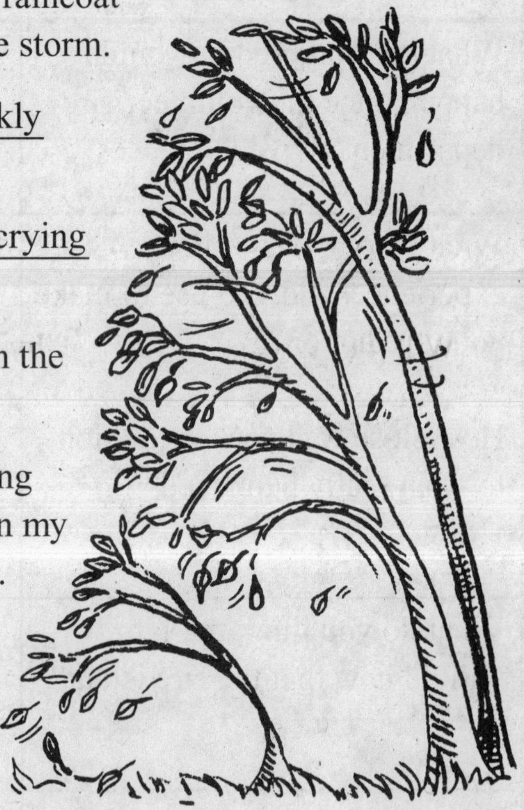

Write a Weather Report

A big storm is coming! On a separate sheet of paper, write a weather report that describes the storm. Use as many vocabulary words as you can.

© Scott Foresman 3

Notes for Home: Your child identified and used vocabulary words from *Brave Irene*. ***Home Activity:*** Play charades with your child. Write the vocabulary words on slips of paper and put them in a bag. Take turns picking out words and acting them out for one another.

Name matt

#1

Predicting

- To **predict** means to tell what you think might happen next in a story based on what has already happened. A prediction is what you say will happen.
- As you read, use what you know from your own life and from what you've learned and look for clues in the story that help you decide what might happen next.

Directions: Reread what happens in *Brave Irene* when she tries to deliver the dress to the duchess. Then answer the questions below.

It really was cold outside, very cold. The wind whirled the falling snowflakes about, this way, that way, and into Irene's squinting face. She set out on the uphill path to Farmer Bennett's sheep pasture.

By the time she got there, the snow was up to her ankles and the wind was worse. It hurried her along and made her stumble. Irene resented this; the box was problem enough. "Easy does it!" she cautioned the wind, leaning back hard against it.

Excerpt from BRAVE IRENE by William Steig. Copyright © 1986 by William Steig. Reprinted by permission of Farrar, Straus & Giroux, Inc.

1. How will the snow affect Irene's trip? It would effect her bad because she would need to put a heavy coat on and it would slow her down.

2. Will the snow get deeper? Why or why not? yes because it keeps pling on.

3. Is the box going to help Irene or make her trip harder? Yes becaus it's hard to carry something big while running.

4. Will saying "Easy does it!" make the wind stop blowing? Why or why not? No because wind can't hear.

5. Tell one of the predictions you made while reading the story and explain whether you had to change this prediction as you continued reading.

© Scott Foresman 3

Notes for Home: Your child read a story and predicted events based on what he or she read. ***Home Activity:*** Watch a TV show with your child. When the show is halfway over, have each person predict its ending. Read these predictions aloud when the show is over.

Test-Taking Tips

1. Write your name on the test.
2. Read the directions carefully. Make sure you know exactly what you are supposed to do.
3. Read the question twice. Make sure you understand what the question is asking.
4. Read the answer choices for the question. Eliminate choices that do not make sense.
5. Mark your answer carefully.
6. Check your answer. Make sure that it makes the most sense out of all the answer choices.
7. If you have difficulty answering a question, you may want to go on to the next question. You can come back to difficult questions later.
8. If you finish the test early, go back and check all your answers.

© Scott Foresman 3

Selection Test

Directions: Choose the best answer to each item. Mark the space for the answer you have chosen.

Part 1: Vocabulary

Find the answer choice that means about the same as the underlined word in each sentence.

1. I was wakened by something howling.
- falling
- making a bright light
- shaking
- making a loud cry

2. The wind knocked down a tree.
- moving air
- truck
- rain
- animal

3. Did that man stumble?
- ask a question
- walk in an unsteady way
- steal something
- drop something

4. My uncle whirled me.
- showed off
- led carefully
- moved round and round
- spoke a name to

5. Jane whipped off her hat.
- poured water
- passed over
- made darker
- pulled quickly

6. The dog snatched the bone.
- chewed
- hid
- found
- grabbed

Part 2: Comprehension

Use what you know about the story to answer each item.

7. Why doesn't Mrs. Bobbin take the dress to the duchess?
- She is lazy.
- She hates to go out in the cold.
- She wants Irene to go to the ball.
- She is sick.

8. What does Irene do just before she gets dressed to go outside?
- She tries on the dress.
- She tucks her mother in bed.
- She tells the wind to be quiet.
- She finishes making the dress.

© Scott Foresman 3

GO ON

9. Why does Irene keep going after the wind warns her to go home?
- She wants to help her mother.
- She doesn't want to get into trouble with her mother.
- She doesn't know the storm is a bad one.
- She wants to run away from home.

10. When the dress blows away, what thought makes Irene most upset?
- She has come out in the storm for nothing.
- Her mother will make her explain to the duchess.
- All her mother's hard work will go to waste.
- Now the duchess will not have fun at her party.

11. A reader is most likely to predict that Irene may die when she—
- remembers her mother's good smell.
- jumps on the box.
- falls off the cliff.
- sees the missing dress.

12. When Irene sees the brightly lit house, a reader is most likely to predict that she will—
- never go home again.
- soon be safe and warm.
- find the dress in the snow.
- go sledding.

13. What lesson does this story teach?
- Never play in the snow.
- Children should never go out alone.
- Life is unfair.
- You should never give up.

14. Irene shows that she is smart when she—
- yells at the wind.
- twists her ankle.
- uses the box as a sled.
- dances at the ball.

15. Which sentence gives an opinion?
- When Mrs. Bobbin woke up, Irene was missing.
- Irene was asleep in the sleigh.
- The duchess sent Irene's mother a ginger cake.
- That is the most beautiful dress in the world.

STOP

© Scott Foresman 3

Text Structure and Graphic Sources

REVIEW

Directions: Read the article and look at the picture. Then read each question about the article and picture. Choose the best answer to the question. Mark the space for the answer you have chosen.

Girl Saves Cat Trapped in Snow

Caitlin Smith of Wildflower Road was walking home from school yesterday afternoon when she heard something crying. She thought something might be trapped in the snow.

She found the spot where she heard the sound and began to dig in the snow. "I reached in and pulled out a cat!" Caitlin said. "The poor thing was wet and cold, and it wouldn't stop crying."

Caitlin brought the cat to the vet. If no one claims the cat, Caitlin's parents say she can keep her.

Caitlin Smith dug this hole to free the trapped cat.

1. The article tells about—
   - ⬭ Wildflower Road.
   - ⬭ the dangers of snow.
   - ⬭ how to care for your pet.
   - ⬬ a girl's rescue of a cat.

2. The author of this article—
   - ⬭ used Caitlin's words.
   - ⬬ made up a story.
   - ⬭ guessed what happened.
   - ⬭ found the cat.

3. This story tells what happened—
   - ⬭ in a mixed-up order.
   - ⬭ last week.
   - ⬬ in the order that the events occurred.
   - ⬭ in a backward order.

4. The picture shows—
   - ⬭ Caitlin's house.
   - ⬭ Caitlin's school.
   - ⬭ how the cat got trapped.
   - ⬬ the hole that Caitlin dug.

5. This article probably appeared—
   - ⬭ in a local newspaper.
   - ⬭ in a school textbook.
   - ⬭ on a neighborhood sign.
   - ⬬ in a storybook.

© Scott Foresman 3

Notes for Home: Your child reviewed elements of text structure. ***Home Activity:*** Read a newspaper or magazine article with your child. Talk about how the author interviews real people and reports what they say in order to tell the story.

Name ______________________

Word Study: Prefixes *im-, dis-, non-*

Directions: Add the prefix **im-, dis-,** or **non-** to each base word. Write the new word formed on the line.

1. im- + possible = imposible

2. dis- + appear = disappear

3. non- + sense = nonsense

4. im- + perfect = imperfect

5. dis- + able = disable

Directions: Choose the word from the box that best fits each definition. Write the word on the line.

disagree
disappear
impossible
imperfect
nonsense

nonsense **6.** something that does not make sense

impossible **7.** not possible

nonperfect **8.** not perfect

disagree **9.** not agree

disappear **10.** no longer in sight

Directions: Add the prefix **im-, dis-,** or **non-** to the base word in ( ) to complete each sentence. Write the word on the line.

nonfiction **11.** I like to read (fiction) books about real-life adventurers at the library.

impatient **12.** Sometimes I get (patient) because I can't wait to get to the end of the book.

disobey **13.** When I'm at the library, I try not to (obey) the rules.

impolite **14.** People who talk in the library are very (polite).

nonsence **15.** The librarian is quick to stop such (sense).

© Scott Foresman 3

Notes for Home: Your child reviewed words with the prefixes *im-, dis-,* and *non-*. ***Home Activity:*** Ask your child to choose words from the box above and use each of them in a sentence. Then ask your child to remove the prefix from each word and use the new word in a sentence.

Name ____________________

REVIEW

Word Study: Plurals

Directions: Read each sentence. Say the underlined word in each sentence. Choose the word that is the plural form of the underlined word. Mark the space for the answer you have chosen.

1. My mother made a stitch.
- stitchs
- stitches
- stitching
- stitch's

2. The branch fell from the tree.
- branch's
- branchs
- branched
- branches

3. I hurt my foot playing soccer.
- feet
- foots
- feets
- foot's

4. My brother has a new tooth.
- toothes
- tooths
- teeth
- teethes

5. A snowflake has six sides.
- snowflakes
- snowflakes'
- snowflaks
- snowflakess

6. John broke his ankle.
- ankle's
- angles
- ankles
- anklees

7. My dad once broke his hand.
- handes
- hands
- handsome
- hands'

8. I have two fish.
- fish
- fishies
- fishs
- fish's

9. Put the book on the shelf.
- shelfs
- shelves
- shelfes
- shelves'

10. The wolf howled.
- wolfs
- wolfes
- wolves
- wolf's

© Scott Foresman 3

Notes for Home: Your child reviewed plurals—words that name more than one person, place, or thing. ***Home Activity:*** Point to a single object in the room, such as a chair. Have your child say and spell the plural form of that word *(chairs)*.

Name ______________________________

Take Notes/Record Findings

Taking notes as you read and **recording findings** of important information can help you better understand what you read. There is no one correct way to take notes. You may wish to organize your notes by topics, by main ideas and supporting details, or as answers to questions you've asked yourself before reading.

Directions: Look at the lists below. Read the paragraph and highlight or underline important information as you read. Then record your findings in the lists.

In the Northeast, winter is a cold time of year. People bundle up in warm clothes. They wear heavy jackets, hats, mittens, and boots. Children like to play outdoors, especially when it snows. They can build snow sculptures and jump in the powdery snow. Other winter activities include skiing, sledding, and ice-skating. After being out in the cold, a cup of hot chocolate, a bowl of hot soup, or a hot bath can warm a cold body.

Clothes	Outdoor Activities	Ways to Warm Up
heavy jackets	build snow sculptures	hot chocolate
hats	jump in snow	hot soup
1. mittens	sledding	5. hot bath
2. boots	3. skiing	
	4. ice-skating	

© Scott Foresman 3

Notes for Home: Your child read a paragraph and recorded important information about it. ***Home Activity:*** Help your child choose a paragraph from a nonfiction book or encyclopedia. Have your child take notes about important information in the paragraph.

Name ______________________________

Author's Purpose

- The **author's purpose** is the author's reason for writing.
- An author may try to express or to describe something in a way that gives the reader a feeling about or sets the mood of the scene.
- An author may try to entertain the reader.

Directions: Reread "Tomás Visits the Library." Then complete the web. Write five story details that the author uses to set the mood of the scene.

Details That Set the Mood

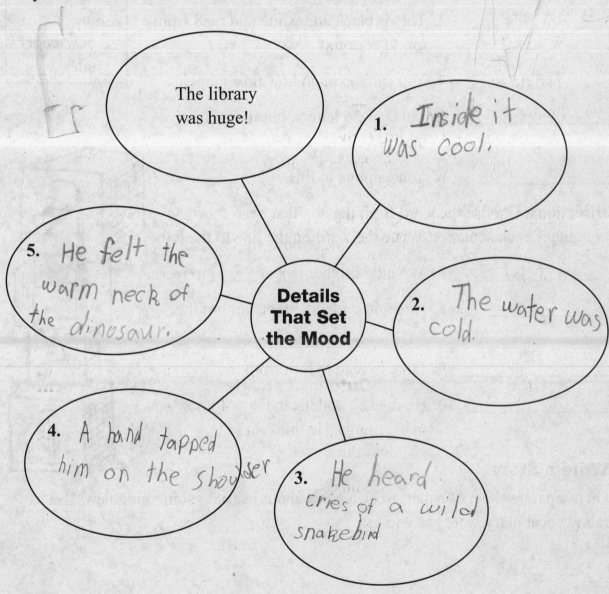

The library was huge!

1. Inside it was cool.
2. The water was cold.
3. He heard cries of a wild snakebird
4. A hand tapped him on the shoulder
5. He felt the warm neck of the dinosaur.

© Scott Foresman 3

Notes for Home: Your child identified details that the author uses to set the mood of a scene. ***Home Activity:*** Work together to write a scary story. Use details that help set a scary mood.

Name ______________________________

Vocabulary

Directions: Choose the word from the box that best matches each clue. Write the word on the line to the left.

Check the Words You Know

- ✓ alphabet
- __ cabin
- ✓ learning
- ✓ magic
- __ newspaper
- __ tales

learning **1.** This activity helps you get smarter.

tales **2.** These sometimes begin "Once upon a time."

newspaper **3.** This is black and white and read from top to bottom.

magic **4.** You can't explain how this happens.

alphebet **5.** This has 26 letters, but it is not a mailbox.

cabin **6.** You can live in this.

Directions: Choose the word from the box that best completes each sentence. Write the word on the line to the left.

learning **7.** My little brother is just _____ to read.

alphebet **8.** He knows a few letters, but not the whole _____.

newspaper **9.** I like to read to him from the _____.

magic **10.** He doesn't understand how I know so many things. He thinks it's _____.

Write a Story

On a separate sheet of paper, write a story about learning something new. Use as many vocabulary words as you can.

© Scott Foresman 3

Notes for Home: Your child identified and used vocabulary words from *More Than Anything Else*. ***Home Activity:*** Help your child write a poem using the vocabulary words listed above.

Name ______________________________

Author's Purpose

- The **author's purpose** is the author's reason for writing.
- An author may try to express or to describe something in a way that gives the reader a feeling about or sets the mood of the scene.
- An author may try to entertain the reader.

Directions: Reread what happens in *More Than Anything Else* when the boy tries to teach himself the alphabet. Then answer the questions below.

I draw the marks on the dirt floor and try to figure out what sounds they make, what story their picture tells.

But sometimes I feel I am trying to jump without legs. And my thoughts get slippery, and I can't keep up with what I want to be, and how good I will feel when I learn this magic, and how people will look up to me.

I can't catch the tune of what I see. I get a salt-shoveling pain and feel my dreams are slipping away.

I have got to find him—that newspaper man.

I look everywhere.

Finally I find that brown face of hope.

He tells me the song—the sounds the marks make.

I jump up and down singing it. I shout and laugh like when I was baptized in the creek. I have jumped into another world and I am saved.

From MORE THAN ANYTHING ELSE by Marie Bradby, illustrated by Chris Soentpiet. Text copyright © 1995 by Marie Bradby. Reprinted by permission of the publisher, Orchard Books, New York.

1. Describe the mood of this passage. ______________________________

____

2. What phrase do you think best describes the boy's frustration?

____

3. List five words from the last paragraph that show the boy's excitement.

____

4. Why does the author call the newspaper man "that brown face of hope"?

____

5. The author compares reading to singing. How does this description make you feel about reading? Explain your feelings on a separate sheet of paper.

© Scott Foresman 3

Notes for Home: Your child read a story and identified details the author uses to set the mood of a scene. ***Home Activity:*** Discuss different types of writing with your child. Talk about different reasons why an author might write a particular kind of writing.

Test-Taking Tips

1. Write your name on the test.
2. Read the directions carefully. Make sure you know exactly what you are supposed to do.
3. Read the question twice. Make sure you understand what the question is asking.
4. Read the answer choices for the question. Eliminate choices that do not make sense.
5. Mark your answer carefully.
6. Check your answer. Make sure that it makes the most sense out of all the answer choices.
7. If you have difficulty answering a question, you may want to go on to the next question. You can come back to difficult questions later.
8. If you finish the test early, go back and check all your answers.

© Scott Foresman 3

Name ____________________

Selection Test

Directions: Choose the best answer to each item. Mark the space for the answer you have chosen.

Part 1: Vocabulary

Find the answer choice that means about the same as the underlined word in each sentence.

1. He is a man of great learning.
- ⬭ strong feeling
- ⬭ knowledge gained by study
- ⬭ places to visit
- ⬭ deep worries and troubles

2. The woman bought a newspaper.
- ⬭ sheets of paper that tell what happened that day
- ⬭ hat to keep the sun off your head
- ⬭ something to clean up spills
- ⬭ cold meal

3. My brother knows the alphabet.
- ⬭ words to a song
- ⬭ the letters of a language in order
- ⬭ answer to a math problem
- ⬭ way to get somewhere

4. Uncle Fred is building a cabin.
- ⬭ wooden boat
- ⬭ large bridge
- ⬭ small house
- ⬭ kind of wagon

5. She has a book of tales.
- ⬭ poems
- ⬭ pictures
- ⬭ songs
- ⬭ stories

6. I love the magic of the woods.
- ⬭ strange power that can make impossible things happen
- ⬭ long war
- ⬭ animals that live in water
- ⬭ business of making food

Part 2: Comprehension

Use what you know about the selection to answer each item.

7. What does the boy do every morning?
- ⬭ goes to school
- ⬭ goes to work
- ⬭ stays at home
- ⬭ catches frogs

8. What does Booker think about all day?
- ⬭ getting more food
- ⬭ getting more money
- ⬭ going to sleep
- ⬭ learning to read

GO ON

© Scott Foresman 3

9. Which sentence best describes Booker?
   - ⬭ He only wants to have fun.
   - ⬭ He is very small for his age.
   - ⬭ He works very hard.
   - ⬭ He changes his mind often.

10. Why does Booker feel hopeful after seeing the man read the newspaper?
   - ⬭ The man smiles at him.
   - ⬭ The newspaper is funny.
   - ⬭ The man has brown skin and knows how to read.
   - ⬭ Suddenly Booker knows how to read.

11. Booker feels as if he is trying to jump without any legs when he tries to—
   - ⬭ teach himself to read.
   - ⬭ catch a frog.
   - ⬭ find the man with the newspaper.
   - ⬭ work on the salt pile.

12. The author's purpose in this selection is to—
   - ⬭ tell how Booker feels about reading.
   - ⬭ tell a funny story about a boy.
   - ⬭ teach people how to read.
   - ⬭ show how letters were first made.

13. The writer wrote this selection as if the boy is telling his story because she wanted to make you—
   - ⬭ think the boy really wrote it.
   - ⬭ understand how the boy feels.
   - ⬭ think the events are taking place right now.
   - ⬭ wish you lived like the boy.

14. What does the author of this selection believe about reading?
   - ⬭ It is everybody's favorite thing to do.
   - ⬭ It wastes time that kids should spend on working.
   - ⬭ It is an important skill to have.
   - ⬭ It wastes time that kids should spend on playing.

15. The man probably teaches Booker how to spell his name because Booker needs to—
   - ⬭ write his name at school.
   - ⬭ know his name if he gets lost.
   - ⬭ write his name at work.
   - ⬭ see the letters work in a way that he can understand.

STOP

© Scott Foresman 3

Fact and Opinion

REVIEW

Directions: Read the letter to the newspaper editor. Then read each question about the letter. Choose the best answer to the question. Mark the space for the answer you have chosen.

Dear Editor,

First, I want to say that I think this is the best newspaper. Everyone should read it. I am the town librarian. I am writing to tell people that next week is literacy week at the library. Literacy means being able to read.

The library will be giving away books, holding classes, and signing people up for membership. The week will be all about reading! It will be fun for everyone. In fact, I think it is the best thing we've ever done here. Reading is fun for all.

Sincerely,
Ms. Elizabeth Perrara

1. Which statement is a statement of fact?
- This is the best newspaper.
- Everyone should read it.
- The library will be giving away books.
- I think this is the best thing we've done.

2. Which statement is a statement of opinion?
- Literacy means being able to read.
- Reading is fun for all.
- I am the librarian.
- Next week is literacy week.

3. This letter—
- lists facts and opinions.
- tells one opinion.
- tells only facts.
- tells only opinions.

4. Why do you think Ms. Perrara wrote this letter?
- She wants people to get involved in literacy week.
- She likes newspapers.
- She knows how to read.
- She is angry about something.

5. How could you best check the facts in this letter?
- by buying a newspaper
- by calling the library
- by asking a friend
- by helping someone learn to read

© Scott Foresman 3

Notes for Home: Your child identified statements of fact and opinion. ***Home Activity:*** Look through the newspaper with your child. Help your child identify statements of fact and opinion in simple articles or letters to the editor.

Name ______________________________

Word Study: Inflected Endings

Directions: Add **-ed** and **-ing** to each word on the left. Remember that you may have to double the last consonant, drop the final **e,** or change **y** to **i.** The first one is done for you.

Word	-ed	-ing
hop	hopped	hopping
1. lift	________	________
2. jump	________	________
3. decide	________	________
4. study	________	________
5. stop	________	________

Directions: Add **-er** and **-est** to each word on the left. Remember that you may have to double the last consonant, drop the final **e,** or change **y** to **i.** The first one is done for you.

Word	-er	-est
funny	funnier	funniest
6. soft	________	________
7. fast	________	________
8. happy	________	________
9. tall	________	________
10. big	________	________

Notes for Home: Your child wrote words that ended with *-ed, -ing, -er,* and *-est.* ***Home Activity:*** Name five words with these endings. Encourage your child to write these words in sentences. Invite your child to write a story with these sentences.

© Scott Foresman 3

Name ______________________________

Phonics: Consonant /k/ Spelled *c, ck, ch*

REVIEW

Directions: Read each sentence. Say the underlined word in each sentence. Choose the word that has the same consonant sound /k/ as the underlined word. Mark the space for the answer you have chosen.

1. My uncle lives in a log <u>cabin</u>.
- cow
- cereal
- chair
- dance

2. Would you like some <u>corn</u>?
- cent
- come
- cheese
- race

3. We have to <u>pack</u> for the trip.
- each
- certain
- neck
- chest

4. Mom patted me on the <u>back</u>.
- cellar
- anchor
- voice
- cheap

5. Does your tooth <u>ache</u>?
- branch
- choir
- ash
- face

6. Please be <u>careful</u>.
- coal
- lace
- lunch
- chop

7. I learned a cool <u>trick</u>.
- sincere
- scent
- charm
- sack

8. Will you sing in the <u>chorus</u>?
- locker
- cement
- church
- chimney

9. I love vanilla ice cream <u>cones</u>.
- chimp
- traces
- cap
- peach

10. Blue is my favorite <u>color</u>.
- chill
- camp
- chase
- nice

© Scott Foresman 3

Notes for Home: Your child reviewed words with the consonant sound /k/ spelled *c, ck,* and *ch*. ***Home Activity:*** Work with your child to make up a poem that uses several words with the consonant sound /k/ spelled *c, ck,* and *ch*.

Name ______________________________

Evaluate Information/Draw Conclusions

Evaluating information means deciding if it is reliable and valid. Ask yourself if the information is complete, factual, and up-to-date. **Drawing conclusions** means thinking about what you have learned from the information and telling what the information means or shows.

Directions: Read the encyclopedia entry. Then answer the questions below.

Mann, Horace
(born May 4, 1796–died August 2, 1859)

Horace Mann grew up in a poor family. He did not attend school on a regular basis. At a young age, Mann educated himself by studying at his local public library in Franklin, Massachusetts. After his graduation from Brown University, Mann became a lawyer. He served in the Massachusetts State House of Representatives and in the Massachusetts Senate.

In 1837, he helped establish a state board of education, which helped improve public education. He believed that everyone deserved a free, quality education.

1. What kinds of information does this passage give about Horace Mann?

____

2. Is this a reliable source for information about Horace Mann? Explain.

____

____

3. Is this information up-to-date? Explain. ______________________________

____

4. Was Horace Mann a hard worker or a lazy person? Why do you think that?

____

____

5. Did Horace Mann believe that poor people deserved the same education as wealthy people? How do you know?

____

____

Notes for Home: Your child read a passage and used it to evaluate and draw conclusions about its information. ***Home Activity:*** Discuss the reliability of different kinds of reference sources with your child, such as encyclopedias, newspapers, magazines, and ads.

© Scott Foresman 3

Name ___________________________________

Plot

- A story's **plot** includes the important events of the story that happen in the beginning, middle, and end of a story.
- Look for events that are important to the plot. They help keep the story going.
- A story map can help you keep track of the most important events in a story.

Beginning → Middle → End

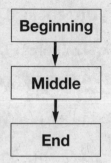

Directions: Reread "Chiefy Stays Over." Then complete the table. List five important story events that happen in the beginning, middle, and end of the story.

Story Section	Important Story Events
Beginning	**1.**
	2.
Middle	**3.**
	4.
End	**5.**

© Scott Foresman 3

Notes for Home: Your child identified important events in a story. ***Home Activity:*** Read a story with your child. Ask him or her to tell you what important events occur at the beginning, middle, and end of the story.

Name ____

Vocabulary

Directions: Draw a line to match each word with its definition.

1. chores	fine, dry dirt
2. pasture	moving very fast
3. dust	small tasks done regularly
4. swift	a kind of small horse
5. pony	a grassy field or hillside
6. saddle	a seat for a rider

Check the Words You Know

- __ chores
- __ dust
- __ pasture
- __ pony
- __ saddle
- __ sturdy
- __ swift

Directions: Cross out the word in each group that does **not** belong.

7. sturdy	strong	weak
8. lazy	swift	fast
9. pasture	field	city
10. chores	jobs	vacation

Write a Letter

Imagine you went horseback riding with your family. On a separate sheet of paper, write a letter to a friend about your adventures. Use as many vocabulary words as you can.

Notes for Home: Your child identified and used vocabulary words from *Leah's Pony*. ***Home Activity:*** Ask your child to pretend he or she is a horse. Encourage your child to write a story from a horse's point of view, using as many vocabulary words as possible.

© Scott Foresman 3

Name ______________________________

Plot

- A story's **plot** includes the important events of the story that happen in the beginning, middle, and end of a story.
- Look for events that are important to the plot. They help keep the story going.

Directions: Reread what happens in *Leah's Pony* when Leah decides to sell her pony. Then answer the questions below about this important story event.

Leah knew what an auction meant. She knew eager faces with strange voices would come to their farm. They would stand outside and offer money for Papa's best bull and Mama's prize rooster and Leah's favorite calf.

All week Leah worried and waited and wondered what to do. One morning she watched as a man in a big hat hammered a sign into the ground in front of her house.

Leah wanted to run away. She raced her pony past empty fields lined with dry gullies. She galloped past a house with rags stuffed in broken windowpanes. She sped right past Mr. B. sweeping the steps outside his store.

At last Leah knew what she had to do. She turned her pony around and rode back into town. She stopped in front of Mr. B.'s store. "You can buy my pony," she said.

From LEAH'S PONY by Elizabeth Friedrich. Text copyright © 1996 by Elizabeth Friedrich. Illustrations copyright © 1996 Michael Garland. Reprinted by permission of Boyds Mills Press.

1. How does the auction make Leah feel? ______________________

____

2. What do those feelings make her do? ______________________

____

3. Who does Leah see while she is out riding her pony? ____________

4. What idea does that give her? ______________________

____

____

5. On a separate sheet of paper, list the important events that take place in the beginning, middle, and end of *Leah's Pony.*

© Scott Foresman 3

Notes for Home: Your child read a story and identified important story events. ***Home Activity:*** Pick a favorite story. Have your child describe important story events from the beginning, middle, and end of the story. Together, draw pictures of some of these events.

Name ________________________________

Test-Taking Tips

1. Write your name on the test.
2. Read the directions carefully. Make sure you know exactly what you are supposed to do.
3. Read the question twice. Make sure you understand what the question is asking.
4. Read the answer choices for the question. Eliminate choices that do not make sense.
5. Mark your answer carefully.
6. Check your answer. Make sure that it makes the most sense out of all the answer choices.
7. If you have difficulty answering a question, you may want to go on to the next question. You can come back to difficult questions later.
8. If you finish the test early, go back and check all your answers.

© Scott Foresman 3

Name ____________________

Selection Test

Directions: Choose the best answer to each item. Mark the space for the answer you have chosen.

Part 1: Vocabulary

Find the answer choice that means about the same as the underlined word in each sentence.

1. Put the <u>saddle</u> in the barn.
   - ⬭ seat that goes on a horse's back
   - ⬭ food for a horse
   - ⬭ machine that is used to plant crops
   - ⬭ baby animal

2. That boat is very <u>swift</u>.
   - ⬭ pretty
   - ⬭ old
   - ⬭ fast
   - ⬭ long

3. Lin wants a <u>pony</u> for her birthday.
   - ⬭ dress
   - ⬭ party
   - ⬭ small horse
   - ⬭ pet bird

4. Did you finish your <u>chores</u>?
   - ⬭ short stories
   - ⬭ small jobs
   - ⬭ snacks
   - ⬭ visits

5. There was <u>dust</u> on the table.
   - ⬭ leftover food
   - ⬭ paper
   - ⬭ water
   - ⬭ fine, dry earth

6. I walked through the <u>pasture</u>.
   - ⬭ grassy field
   - ⬭ large building
   - ⬭ small stream
   - ⬭ thick woods

7. Jack is a <u>sturdy</u> boy.
   - ⬭ smart
   - ⬭ hungry
   - ⬭ rude
   - ⬭ strong

Part 2: Comprehension

Use what you know about the story to answer each item.

8. Who bought the pony for Leah?
   - ⬭ Mama
   - ⬭ Papa
   - ⬭ Mr. B.
   - ⬭ the neighbors

© Scott Foresman 3

GO ON

9. What did Mr. B. always say about Leah's pony?
- ⬭ It was the finest in the county.
- ⬭ It was too small for her.
- ⬭ He wanted it for his grandson.
- ⬭ Leah should sell it.

10. The beginning of this story is mostly about how—
- ⬭ the corn grew tall.
- ⬭ Leah sold her pony.
- ⬭ Leah's family held an auction.
- ⬭ Leah first got and rode her pony.

11. What happened just after the grasshoppers came?
- ⬭ The neighbors moved away.
- ⬭ Leah got a new pony.
- ⬭ Papa sold the pigs.
- ⬭ Leah sold her pony.

12. The ending is mostly about how—
- ⬭ Leah's family moved to Oregon.
- ⬭ Mama and Papa began to worry.
- ⬭ Leah's family's farm was saved.
- ⬭ Papa decided to sell the tractor.

13. What was the main problem with the farm?
- ⬭ There was not enough rain.
- ⬭ There was no one to work.
- ⬭ The weather was too cold.
- ⬭ The farm animals were sick.

14. Leah's decision about the pony shows that the most important thing to her was—
- ⬭ learning to ride the tractor.
- ⬭ staying friendly with Mr. B.
- ⬭ making lots of money.
- ⬭ helping her family.

15. What lesson does this story teach?
- ⬭ Most problems are solved with good luck.
- ⬭ People can solve problems by helping one another.
- ⬭ Only rich, important people can solve problems.
- ⬭ It's better to accept a big problem than to try to fix it.

STOP

© Scott Foresman 3

Theme

REVIEW

Directions: Read the story. Then read each question about the story. Choose the best answer to the question. Mark the space for the answer you have chosen.

Worthwhile

Patti sighed as she looked around her horse's stall. Cinnamon needed fresh straw, food, and water.

Patti began raking out the dirty straw. Her hands hurt and her shoulders ached. This part of owning a horse was hard work!

Patti got Cinnamon's curry comb and brush. "Remember how we rode to Liz's house yesterday?" she asked Cinnamon as she brushed. "It was such a pretty ride through the woods. I wish that we could spend the entire day together."

Patti thought about her life before Cinnamon arrived. "Maybe I had more free time then, and I didn't have to do things like clean up dirty straw," she said. "But you know what? I don't mind doing these things if it means I have you to ride."

1. At the beginning of the story, Patti is unhappy because she—
- ⬭ doesn't like horses.
- ⬭ wants to ride Cinnamon.
- ⬭ has many chores to do.
- ⬭ is mad at Cinnamon.

2. Raking out the dirty straw—
- ⬭ is hard, unpleasant work.
- ⬭ is easy to do.
- ⬭ is Patti's favorite job.
- ⬭ only takes a few minutes.

3. As Patti brushes Cinnamon, she—
- ⬭ is in a bad mood.
- ⬭ wishes she could spend less time riding.
- ⬭ doesn't say a word.
- ⬭ thinks about what having a horse means.

4. Before getting Cinnamon, Patti—
- ⬭ had more free time.
- ⬭ didn't like horses.
- ⬭ went riding with Liz.
- ⬭ had more fun.

5. The theme of this story is that—
- ⬭ riding is fun.
- ⬭ horses are too much work.
- ⬭ Patti likes Cinnamon.
- ⬭ horses are a lot of work, but they are worth it.

© Scott Foresman 3

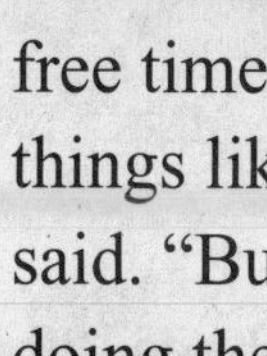

Notes for Home: Your child identified the theme of a story. ***Home Activity:*** Read a book or watch a video with your child. Ask what the theme, or big idea, of the book or video is. Talk about what lessons about life can be learned from it.

Phonics: Consonant Digraph *wh*; Consonant /h/ Spelled *wh*

Directions: Circle each word with **wh** that has the same beginning sound as **who** or **where.** Then write each word in the correct column.

1. Liz whispered to Bob about why she was excited.
2. Later, she told the whole class about what she hoping to do.
3. Liz wanted to have fundraisers which would help buy a new wheelchair ramp.
4. When Liz said, "Whoever raises the most will win a prize," we cheered.
5. "Who'll help me out?" Liz asked. "Who's ready to have an auction?"

who	**where**
6. ______________	10. ______________
7. ______________	11. ______________
8. ______________	12. ______________
9. ______________	13. ______________
	14. ______________
	15. ______________

Directions: Cross out the word that does **not** have the same beginning sound as the first word.

16. who	whom	somewhat	whose
17. what	why	where	wholesome
18. which	whip	white	whoever
19. whole	whose	who'll	whale
20. while	whenever	who'd	whether

Notes for Home: Your child reviewed words with *wh*. ***Home Activity:*** Write words beginning with *wh* on slips of paper and put them in a hat or bowl. Ask your child to pull out each piece of paper and pronounce the word correctly.

© Scott Foresman 3

Word Study: Prefixes *im-, dis-, non-*

REVIEW

Directions: Read each sentence. Say the underlined word in each sentence. Choose the word that means the opposite of the underlined word. Mark the space for the answer you have chosen.

1. I try to be patient when I have to wait.
- calm
- impatient
- disappointed
- relaxed

2. Lee's cat appeared last night.
- disappeared
- returned
- apples
- reappeared

3. This song makes sense.
- funny
- silly
- sad
- nonsense

4. This flight will stop.
- fast
- slow
- nonstop
- important

5. It is polite to thank people.
- nice
- impolite
- good
- disloyal

6. It is possible to fix it.
- broken
- easy
- impossible
- disobey

7. I agree with you.
- agreement
- nonsense
- disagree
- anger

8. Do you like this music?
- dislike
- love
- disbelieve
- distant

9. I trust you.
- trusted
- disagree
- believe
- distrust

10. Your drawing is perfect.
- dirty
- perfectly
- imperfect
- important

© Scott Foresman 3

Notes for Home: Your child reviewed words with the prefixes *im-, dis-,* and *non-*. ***Home Activity:*** Write pairs of words with one of these three prefixes added to one word, such as *obey* and *disobey*. Discuss how adding the prefix changes the meaning of the base word.

Name ______________________________

Time Line/Chart/Table

A **time line** shows events in the order that they happened or will happen. A **chart** organizes information in a form that is easy to understand, such as a list, table, or diagram. A **table** is a kind of chart that shows information in rows and columns so it is easy to compare.

Directions: Look at the time line. Use the time line to answer the questions.

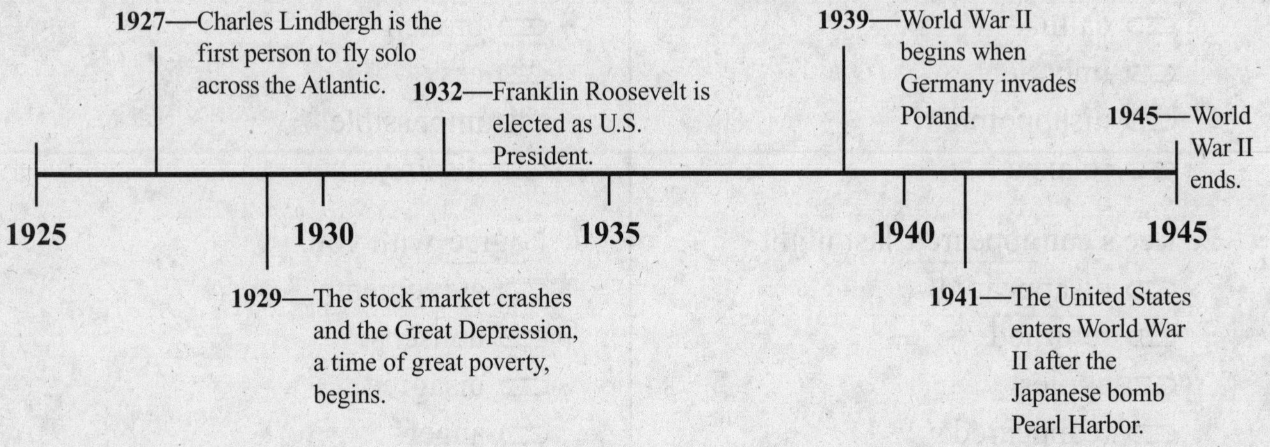

1927—Charles Lindbergh is the first person to fly solo across the Atlantic.
1929—The stock market crashes and the Great Depression, a time of great poverty, begins.
1932—Franklin Roosevelt is elected as U.S. President.
1939—World War II begins when Germany invades Poland.
1941—The United States enters World War II after the Japanese bomb Pearl Harbor.
1945—World War II ends.
1925
1930
1935
1940
1945

1. What are the first and last years shown on the time line? How many years total does the time line show ?

____

2. When did the Great Depression begin? ______________

3. What major events happened during 1930 to 1940?

____

____

4. How long did World War II last? ______________

5. If you had information about the different roles that different countries played during World War II, would you use a time line or a table to present this information? Explain.

____

____

Notes for Home: Your child read information recorded on a time line and answered questions about it. ***Home Activity:*** Help your child make a time line that highlights important events in his or her life.

© Scott Foresman 3

Name ______________________________

Steps in a Process

- Following **steps in a process** usually means doing or making something in a certain order.
- Sometimes the steps in a process are given in pictures as well as words.
- Sometimes there are clue words, such as *the next step* or *then,* that help you with the order of the steps.

Directions: Reread "Revealing a Pattern." Complete the flowchart. List the steps in order to show how to make a leaf rubbing. Then answer the questions below.

Make a Leaf Rubbing

Find a leaf with a strong vein pattern.

↓

1.

↓

2.

↓

3.

4. What materials do you need to do this project? ______________________________

____

5. What might happen if you skipped a step? ______________________________

____

© Scott Foresman 3

Notes for Home: Your child read a story and put steps in a process in the correct order. ***Home Activity:*** Discuss a favorite activity with your child. Ask him or her to tell you steps that need to be taken in the correct order.

Name ______________________________

Vocabulary

Directions: Choose the word from the box that best fits each definition. Write the word on the line.

Check the Words You Know
__ cone
__ creating
__ designed
__ famous
__ paste
__ swan

______________ **1.** making something that did not exist before

______________ **2.** a mixture used to stick things together

______________ **3.** very well known

______________ **4.** an object with a flat, round base and a pointed top

______________ **5.** a graceful, long-necked bird

______________ **6.** planned out

Directions: Choose the word from the box that best completes each sentence. Write the word on the line to the left.

______________ **7.** In art class I am _____ a sculpture.

______________ **8.** Kerry is good at planning things, so she _____ it with me.

______________ **9.** My sculpture is a _____ with a long, curved neck.

______________ **10.** Perhaps I will become _____ someday for making great art!

Write a Memo

On a separate sheet of paper, write a memo to your art teacher. It should say TO: (your teacher's name) and FROM: (your name). Tell your teacher what things you would like to create in art class. Use as many vocabulary words as you can.

© Scott Foresman 3

Notes for Home Your child identified and used new vocabulary words from *The Piñata Maker. **Home Activity:*** Ask your child to make a list of things he or she enjoys doing in art class. Encourage him or her to use as many vocabulary words as possible.

Name ______________________________

Steps in a Process

- Following **steps in a process** usually means doing or making something in a certain order.
- Sometimes the steps in a process are given in pictures as well as words.
- Sometimes there are clue words, such as *the next step* or *then,* that help you with the order of the steps.

Directions: Reread what happens in *The Piñata Maker* when Tío Rico makes a swan piñata. Then answer the questions below.

He begins by rolling dry banana leaves into a thick rod with a bulge at one end for the head. He wraps the rod in brown paper smeared with paste. Then he forms the neck into an S-shaped curve and places it in the sun. Old irons hold it in shape until it's dry.

Next Tío Rico covers the neck with white paper so the brown won't show through the outer layer of white crepe paper feathers. Then he makes a shallow cardboard cone, cuts it in the center, and glues it onto the base of the neck.

Tío Rico rolls another piece of cardboard into a large cone. He bends the end to form the swan's tail and wraps it.

Excerpt from THE PIÑATA MAKER/EL PIÑATERO, copyright © 1994 by George Ancona, reprinted by permission of Harcourt Brace & Company.

1. What does Tío Rico do first? ______________________________

____

2. What does Tío Rico do so that the brown won't show through the outer layer?

____

3. What does Tío Rico do last? ______________________________

____

4. List the clue words that help you tell the order of the steps. ____________

____

5. Decide what the main steps are in the process of making a piñata. Then draw a picture for each major step.

© Scott Foresman 3

Notes for Home: Your child read a selection and identified the steps in a process. ***Home Activity:*** Cook a meal with your child. Read from a cookbook or recipe and discuss the steps that must be taken in a certain order to prepare the food correctly.

Test-Taking Tips

1. Write your name on the test.
2. Read the directions carefully. Make sure you know exactly what you are supposed to do.
3. Read the question twice. Make sure you understand what the question is asking.
4. Read the answer choices for the question. Eliminate choices that do not make sense.
5. Mark your answer carefully.
6. Check your answer. Make sure that it makes the most sense out of all the answer choices.
7. If you have difficulty answering a question, you may want to go on to the next question. You can come back to difficult questions later.
8. If you finish the test early, go back and check all your answers.

© Scott Foresman 3

Name ______________________________

Selection Test

Directions: Choose the best answer to each item. Mark the space for the answer you have chosen.

Part 1: Vocabulary

Find the answer choice that means about the same as the underlined word in each sentence.

1. Sarah was <u>creating</u> a pot.
- ⊂⊃ filling
- ⊂⊃ copying
- ⊂⊃ making
- ⊂⊃ painting

2. We bought some <u>paste</u>.
- ⊂⊃ special paper
- ⊂⊃ a tool used to apply paint
- ⊂⊃ a mixture used to stick things together
- ⊂⊃ a tool used to cut things

3. Don't get too close to a <u>swan</u>.
- ⊂⊃ large water bird
- ⊂⊃ powerful machine
- ⊂⊃ waterfall
- ⊂⊃ campfire

4. My aunt is <u>famous</u>.
- ⊂⊃ well known
- ⊂⊃ powerful
- ⊂⊃ rich
- ⊂⊃ well educated

5. Kevin wore a <u>cone</u> on his head.
- ⊂⊃ hat with a large brim
- ⊂⊃ shape with a flat, round bottom and a point on top
- ⊂⊃ long, thin piece of cloth
- ⊂⊃ kind of plastic bandage

6. Who <u>designed</u> that house?
- ⊂⊃ bought
- ⊂⊃ made the plan for
- ⊂⊃ built
- ⊂⊃ fixed up

Part 2: Comprehension

Use what you know about the selection to answer each item.

7. What did Don Ricardo do before he started to make piñatas?
- ⊂⊃ He made hats.
- ⊂⊃ He built houses.
- ⊂⊃ He worked with animals.
- ⊂⊃ He taught in a school.

8. Why did Don Ricardo leave his first job?
- ⊂⊃ People begged him to make piñatas.
- ⊂⊃ His job did not pay well.
- ⊂⊃ His job made it hard for him to walk around.
- ⊂⊃ He got fired from his job.

GO ON

© Scott Foresman 3

9. To make paste, Don Ricardo mixes water and—
- ⬭ flour.
- ⬭ clay.
- ⬭ paper.
- ⬭ corn.

10. What part of the swan piñata does Don Ricardo make first?
- ⬭ the neck
- ⬭ the feathers
- ⬭ the body
- ⬭ the feet

11. What does Don Ricardo do with each part of the swan right after he forms it?
- ⬭ paints it
- ⬭ covers it with white paper
- ⬭ puts it in the sun to dry
- ⬭ takes it to the market

12. Which of the following steps does Don Ricardo do last?
- ⬭ sews the wings to the body
- ⬭ buys a pot
- ⬭ makes the feathers
- ⬭ forms the beak out of cardboard

13. What part of the piñata is a pot used for?
- ⬭ the body
- ⬭ the head
- ⬭ the neck
- ⬭ the feet

14. Which sentence best describes Don Ricardo?
- ⬭ He wishes he had another job.
- ⬭ He only cares about money.
- ⬭ He works as fast as possible.
- ⬭ He does fine, careful work.

15. Which sentence gives a fact?
- ⬭ Don Ricardo left school to help his father.
- ⬭ Starch makes the best paste.
- ⬭ Piñatas are fun.
- ⬭ Don Ricardo makes the best piñatas in the world.

STOP

© Scott Foresman 3

Name ______________________________

Generalizing

REVIEW

Directions: Read the story. Then read each question about the story. Choose the best answer to the question. Mark the space for the answer you have chosen.

Super Sombreros

My uncle, Juan Sanchez, makes sombreros. Sombreros are Mexican hats. His sombreros are the most beautiful in all of Mexico. He has been making them since he was thirteen years old. Nobody can make sombreros as well as he can.

Uncle Juan makes each sombrero differently for each person. Everybody knows that this is the only way to make sombreros. He always spends at least a week on each sombrero. Sometimes he takes more time on a hat if it is for a special occasion. Either way, all of his customers are pleased with their specially made sombreros.

1. Which sentence is a generalization?
- ⬭ A sombrero is a Mexican hat.
- ⬭ My uncle makes sombreros.
- ⬭ His sombreros are the most beautiful in all of Mexico.
- ⬭ He has been making them since he was thirteen years old.

2. Which sentence is **not** a generalization?
- ⬭ He has been making them since he was thirteen years old.
- ⬭ Nobody can make sombreros as well as he can.
- ⬭ He always spends a week on each sombrero.
- ⬭ His sombreros are the most beautiful in all of Mexico.

3. Which of the following words signals a generalization in the second paragraph?
- ⬭ always
- ⬭ either
- ⬭ sombreros
- ⬭ pleased

4. Which of the following words does **not** signal a generalization in the second paragraph?
- ⬭ everybody
- ⬭ differently
- ⬭ all
- ⬭ always

5. A generalization about this passage could be—
- ⬭ Juan Sanchez makes sombreros.
- ⬭ The author is proud of her uncle.
- ⬭ Juan Sanchez makes a special hat for each customer.
- ⬭ Juan Sanchez makes the best sombreros in all of Mexico.

© Scott Foresman 3

Notes for Home: Your child reviewed generalizations. ***Home Activity:*** Together with your child, read some short newspaper articles. Ask him or her to point out generalizations. Ask your child to tell you what words helped him or her identify each generalization.

Name ____________________

Phonics: The *Schwa* Sound

Directions: Choose the word with a vowel that has the same sound as the underlined vowels in **about, taken, pencil, lemon,** and **circus** to complete each sentence. Write the word on the line to the left.

__________ **1.** Angela will demonstrate making kites _____.
today Tuesday someday

__________ **2.** She paints her kites with _____ designs.
funny pretty colorful

__________ **3.** Her kites have very _____ shapes.
complicated lovely swooping

__________ **4.** Some are shaped like _____.
doughnuts triangles pinwheels

__________ **5.** She adds bright tassels and _____ to some.
rainbows ribbons rings

__________ **6.** Some are made to look like _____.
butterflies peacocks seashells

__________ **7.** My favorite looks like a _____.
rabbit goldfish dragon

Directions: Circle the letter in each word that stands for the same sound as the underlined vowels in **about, taken, pencil, lemon,** and **circus.**

8. k i t c h e n

9. a g o

10. c a r r o t

11. d i f f i c u l t

12. r i v e r

13. s u r p r i s e

14. a s t r o n a u t

15. p o e m

© Scott Foresman 3

Notes for Home: Your child reviewed words that contain a schwa sound—a sound heard only in unaccented syllables. For example, *ago, kitchen,* and *pencil*. ***Home Activity:*** Work with your child to identify letters that stand for the schwa sound in words such as: *alone, item, mother,*

Name ______________________________

REVIEW

Phonics: Digraph *wh*; /h/ Spelled *wh*

Directions: Read each sentence. Say the underlined word in each sentence. Choose the word that has the same beginning sound as the underlined word. Mark the space for the answer you have chosen.

1. He gave the piñata a whack.
- when
- who
- write
- wrestle

2. The piñata looked like a whale.
- whose
- who
- wheel
- wrench

3. Who will knock it down?
- whole
- will
- whistle
- wheel

4. What is inside?
- who's
- while
- whole
- wrote

5. Who's at the door?
- word
- witness
- which
- whom

6. Where can I put this gift?
- here
- why
- wrapped
- whomever

7. This gift is from whom?
- what
- whose
- window
- winter

8. He got a unicycle with one wheel.
- who
- heel
- whistle
- whole

9. We ate the whole cake.
- we
- well
- why
- hope

10. I loved the white frosting.
- whoever
- high
- who
- where

© Scott Foresman 3

Notes for Home: Your child reviewed words beginning with *wh* that have the consonant sounds in *who* and *white*. ***Home Activity:*** With your child, list words that begin with *wh*. Write them on slips of paper. Then ask your child to sort the words by the sound *wh* represents.

Name ____________________

Diagram

A **diagram** is a special drawing with labels. It usually shows how something is made or how it works.

Directions: Look at the diagram of a sewing machine. Use the diagram to answer the questions.

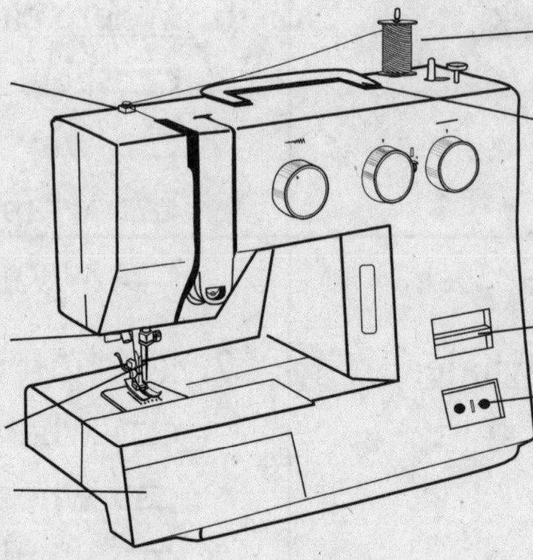

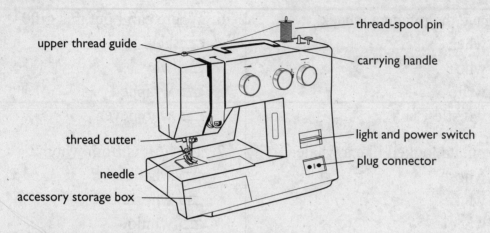

1. How would you turn the sewing machine on and off? ____________________

____

2. Which part is located below the light and power switch? ____________________

____

3. Where does the thread go after it is placed on the thread-spool pin?

____

____

4. Where can extra sewing things be stored? ____________________

____

5. If you were learning how to sew, why would this diagram be helpful?

____

____

© Scott Foresman 3

Notes for Home: Your child used a diagram to answer questions. ***Home Activity:*** Find a simple diagram. Often kitchen appliances or garden tools come with clear diagrams. Have your child look at the diagram and then locate the parts on the actual object.

Name Matt Benson

Setting

- The **setting** is the time and place of a story.
- An author may not always tell you when and where a story takes place. Look for clues in the art or words that point to the setting in the story.
- The setting can determine how a character acts in a story.

Directions: Reread "On the Train." Complete the table. For each place listed, give story details that describe it. Then answer the question below.

Setting	Story Details
Railroad Car	**1.** When train time was called we marched right past the bulging eye
	2.
Land Outside Train	**3.**
	4.

5. Does this story take place in modern times or in the past? Explain.

© Scott Foresman 3

Notes for Home: Your child read a story and identified the setting. ***Home Activity:*** Read a passage from the middle of a story that does not make any direct statements about the setting. Have your child draw conclusions about the setting based on the author's clues.

Name ______________________________________

Vocabulary

Directions: Choose the word from the box that best fits each definition. Write the word on the line.

Check the Words You Know
__ bundled
__ carted
__ conductor
__ label
__ mailing
__ station

____________________ **1.** a slip of paper that is attached to something

____________________ **2.** sending by mail

____________________ **3.** tied or wrapped together

____________________ **4.** the person in charge of a train or bus

Directions: Choose the word from the box that best completes each sentence. Write the word on the line to the left.

____________________ **5.** We _____ our old toys together and wrapped them.

____________________ **6.** We _____ the clothes in our wagon.

____________________ **7.** We walked all the way to the railway _____.

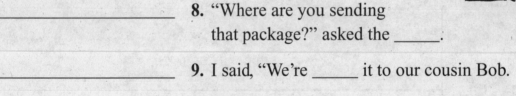

____________________ **8.** "Where are you sending that package?" asked the _____.

____________________ **9.** I said, "We're _____ it to our cousin Bob.

____________________ **10.** I pointed to the _____ that showed Bob's name and address.

Write a Letter

On a separate sheet of paper, write a letter about a trip on a train. It can be a trip you really took, or one you make up. Use as many vocabulary words as you can.

Notes for Home Your child identified and used new vocabulary words from *Mailing May*. ***Home Activity:*** Ask your child to tell you what happens to a letter after it's mailed. Encourage him or her to use as many vocabulary words as possible.

© Scott Foresman 3

Name ______________________________

Setting

- The **setting** is the time and place of a story.
- An author may not always tell you when and where a story takes place. Look for clues in the art or words that point to the setting in the story.
- The setting can determine how a character acts in a story.

Directions: Reread the part of *Mailing May* where Mr. Perkins weighs May. Then answer the questions below.

"Forty-eight pounds and eight ounces. Biggest baby chick on record!" Mr. Perkins ran his finger down a chart hanging near the scale and turned to Pa. "To mail May from Grangeville to Lewiston will cost fifty-three cents. Well, Leonard, looks like you'll be in charge of some poultry on this mail run."

Before I knew it, Mr. Perkins had glued fifty-three cents worth of stamps on the back of my coat. . . .

From MAILING MAY by Michael O. Tunnel. Text Copyright © 1997 by Michael O. Tunnell. By permission of Tambourine Books /Greenwillow Books, divisions of William Morrow & Company, Inc.

1. When do you think this story takes place—in the past or in modern times?

____

2. What clues did you use to figure out when this story takes place?

____

____

3. Where is this scene taking place? ______________________________

____

4. What clues did you use to figure out where this scene takes place?

____

____

5. Pick another scene in the story, such as May's house, what May sees on the train ride, or Grandma Mary's house. Use picture clues and words to help you describe the setting.

© Scott Foresman 3

Notes for Home: Your child read a passage from a story and identified the setting. ***Home Activity:*** With your child, read a scene from a book that is not illustrated. Then ask your child to draw what he or she thinks is the setting from details given in the story.

Test-Taking Tips

1. Write your name on the test.
2. Read the directions carefully. Make sure you know exactly what you are supposed to do.
3. Read the question twice. Make sure you understand what the question is asking.
4. Read the answer choices for the question. Eliminate choices that do not make sense.
5. Mark your answer carefully.
6. Check your answer. Make sure that it makes the most sense out of all the answer choices.
7. If you have difficulty answering a question, you may want to go on to the next question. You can come back to difficult questions later.
8. If you finish the test early, go back and check all your answers.

© Scott Foresman 3

Name ______________________________

Selection Test

Directions: Choose the best answer to each item. Mark the space for the answer you have chosen.

Part 1: Vocabulary

Find the answer choice that means about the same as the underlined word in each sentence.

1. Dad <u>bundled</u> the old clothes.
- ⬭ wrapped together
- ⬭ threw away
- ⬭ sorted into piles
- ⬭ gave away

2. Who <u>carted</u> the kids to the fair?
- ⬭ invited
- ⬭ carried
- ⬭ walked
- ⬭ ordered

3. Workers cleaned up the <u>station</u>.
- ⬭ place where goods are sold
- ⬭ home of a mayor or governor
- ⬭ building where a train picks up passengers
- ⬭ open space in a city

4. Can you read this <u>label</u>?
- ⬭ book in which someone writes
- ⬭ map
- ⬭ slip of paper with a name or address stuck onto a package
- ⬭ letter

5. The <u>conductor</u> greeted us.
- ⬭ person who is having a party
- ⬭ person who runs a school
- ⬭ person in charge of a train or bus
- ⬭ person in charge of a museum

6. Sam was <u>mailing</u> the invitations.
- ⬭ writing out
- ⬭ putting art on
- ⬭ sending through the post office
- ⬭ answering

Part 2: Comprehension

Use what you know about the story to answer each item.

7. Grandma lived in the town of—
- ⬭ Grangeville.
- ⬭ Sweetwater.
- ⬭ Lewiston.
- ⬭ Joseph.

8. At first, May's parents said she could not visit Grandma because—
- ⬭ she was too young.
- ⬭ they couldn't buy a train ticket.
- ⬭ Grandma didn't want visitors.
- ⬭ the train didn't go to Grandma's.

© Scott Foresman 3

GO ON

9. May went to Alexander's Department Store to—
- help Mr. Alexander count money.
- get some candy.
- buy a present for Grandma.
- ask for a job.

10. How can you tell that this story takes place in the winter?
- There is snow on the ground.
- People ride on the train.
- The children are in school.
- May's father has no money.

11. When May first realized that she was being mailed, she was—
- on the train.
- in her kitchen.
- in the department store.
- in the post office.

12. Which part of the story is supposed to make you laugh?
- May's father had to pay 53 cents to send her on the train.
- May and her valise had to weigh less than 50 pounds.
- May had to travel in the mail car.
- May got stamps and a label on her coat.

13. When the conductor first found May on the train, he felt—
- worried.
- shy.
- angry.
- friendly.

14. Which sentence gives details about the setting of this story?
- "He and Ma commenced in whispering and peeking at me off and on."
- "Mr. Perkins looked at me over his glasses and then sniffed."
- "Biggest baby chick on record!"
- "At exactly seven o'clock, the train chugged away from my home and headed down the mountain."

15. In this story, why was it safe for May's parents to send her as a package?
- Ma's cousin Leonard was in charge of the mail on the train.
- Grandma would be so happy to see her.
- Her father rode with her.
- The conductor offered to make sure she was safe on the train.

STOP

© Scott Foresman 3

Name ______________________________

Making Judgments and Character

REVIEW

Directions: Read the story. Then read each question about the story. Choose the best answer to the question. Mark the space for the answer you have chosen.

The Big Trip

"Let's go, Molly!" Tommy yelled. "You're not going to make us late again."

Molly scrambled to catch up. "I thought I forgot my ticket."

Tommy smiled at Molly and rolled his eyes. They found their seats just as the train started to pull out of the station. Both friends sighed with relief. Then they looked for places to put their bags.

Tommy's bag was small and packed with neatly folded clothes. Molly had two bags which were stuffed full. One bag had socks poking out through the zipper.

"Here, Tommy," she said. "I brought you some sports magazines and your favorite gummy bears." Then she pulled out a book to read. Now that they were settled in, they could enjoy the trip!

1. Tommy is—
- ⬭ messy and disorganized.
- ⬭ neat and responsible.
- ⬭ mean and insensitive.
- ⬭ careless and forgetful.

2. What do Tommy's comments tell readers about Molly?
- ⬭ She is never late.
- ⬭ She is not very nice.
- ⬭ She doesn't like Tommy.
- ⬭ She is often late.

3. Tommy and Molly's bags show readers that—
- ⬭ Molly is messy.
- ⬭ Molly is organized.
- ⬭ Tommy is messy.
- ⬭ The two friends are very much alike.

4. From Molly's actions in the last paragraph, readers learn that Molly is—
- ⬭ not nice.
- ⬭ thoughtful and giving.
- ⬭ selfish.
- ⬭ angry with Tommy.

5. Tommy and Molly—
- ⬭ know each other well.
- ⬭ don't like one another.
- ⬭ just met.
- ⬭ are too different to be good friends.

© Scott Foresman 3

Notes for Home: Your child read a story and made judgments about the characters. ***Home Activity:*** Have your child describe a favorite TV character. Ask your child to make a judgment about how that character behaves.

Name ______________________________

Word Study: Syllabication

Directions: Choose the word from the box that best completes each sentence. Write the word on the line to the left. Put a dot between each syllable: **break • fast.**

circus	darkness	mountain	station	uniform
commenced	flabbergasted	scrambled	suddenly	

_____________ **1.** The train left the _____ right on time.

_____________ **2.** Tommy's journey had _____.

_____________ **3.** Tommy was _____ to see a bear coming down the aisle.

_____________ **4.** The bear wore a blue _____ with gold buttons.

_____________ **5.** Apparently there was a _____ traveling on the train.

_____________ **6.** The train entered a tunnel cut into the _____ .

_____________ **7.** Tommy could see nothing in the _____.

_____________ **8.** Something _____ into the seat beside him.

_____________ **9.** A hairy hand _____ tugged on his ear.

Directions: Choose the word from the box that finishes each word below. The last letter in each word is given. Write each syllable of the word on the line.

emergency	neighborhoods
kindness	opposite
meanwhile	yesterday

10. ________ • ________e

11. ________ • ________ • ________e

12. ________ • ________ • ________s

13. ________ • ________s

14. ________ • ________ • ________ • ________y

15. ________ • ________ • ________y

Read the first letter of each word above to find out who Tom's seatmate was.

Answer: ____________

Notes for Home: Your child divided words into syllables, or smaller word parts. ***Home Activity:*** Encourage your child to read challenging books aloud to you, breaking up unfamiliar words into syllables in order to pronounce and understand them better.

© Scott Foresman 3

Word Study: Inflected Endings REVIEW

Directions: Read each sentence. Choose the word that best completes each sentence. Mark the space for the answer you have chosen.

1. It was the _____ train of all.
- ⬭ big
- ⬭ bigger
- ⬭ biggest
- ⬭ huge

2. I _____ to find a seat.
- ⬭ tries
- ⬭ trial
- ⬭ tried
- ⬭ trying

3. We _____ at a big station.
- ⬭ stopper
- ⬭ stops
- ⬭ stopping
- ⬭ stopped

4. Then we _____ for home.
- ⬭ started
- ⬭ starts
- ⬭ staring
- ⬭ starting

5. I was _____ the minutes.
- ⬭ count
- ⬭ counter
- ⬭ counting
- ⬭ counted

6. I was the _____ passenger in the whole train.
- ⬭ happiest
- ⬭ happier
- ⬭ happy
- ⬭ happening

7. My brother was the _____ passenger of all.
- ⬭ younger
- ⬭ young
- ⬭ youngest
- ⬭ most

8. He is _____ than I am.
- ⬭ funny
- ⬭ funnier
- ⬭ funniest
- ⬭ fun

9. Finally, we _____ home.
- ⬭ arrives
- ⬭ arriving
- ⬭ arrived
- ⬭ getting

10. Our parents were _____ for us.
- ⬭ wait
- ⬭ waits
- ⬭ waited
- ⬭ waiting

© Scott Foresman 3

Notes for Home: Your child reviewed words that end in *-ed, -ing, -est,* and *-er*. ***Home Activity:*** Give your child a group of verbs *(jump, play, hop)* and adjectives *(tall, soft, big)*. Have your child add *-ed* and *-ing* to the verbs and *-er* and *-est* to the adjectives.

Name ______________________________

Poster/Advertisement

A **poster** gives information about an event. An **advertisement** is an announcement that tries to persuade readers, listeners, or viewers to do something, buy something, or feel a particular way about something.

Directions: Use the poster advertisement to answer the questions that follow.

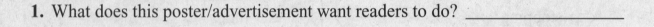

Special Edition Stamps!

For a limited time only, the U.S. Post Office presents "Dinosaur Stamps"!

Available from May 1–July 1 or while supplies last at your local post office.

The first 50 people to buy a book of stamps will get a free movie ticket.

These incredibly realistic stamps are a perfect addition to any collection!

Don't wait because these dinosaurs will soon be extinct!

1. What does this poster/advertisement want readers to do? ______________________________

____

2. Where would you go to buy a book of stamps? ______________________________

3. Even if you didn't need stamps, why might you buy them? ______________________________

____

____

4. What would be the benefit of going to the post office early on May 1?

____

____

5. What words are used to help persuade readers? ______________________________

____

Notes for Home: Your child used a poster advertisement to answer questions. ***Home Activity:*** Have your child create a poster for an upcoming family event. Encourage your child to use the questions: *Who? What? When? Where? How?* to complete the poster.

© Scott Foresman 3

Name ________________________________

Visualizing

- **To visualize** is to create a picture in your mind.
- When you read, you may be able to use the details in the text along with what you know about the subject to see, smell, hear, taste, and feel what the author describes.

Directions: Reread "First Day in London." Complete the two boxes. List details that help you visualize Aunt Pam and Amber.

Aunt Pam	Amber
1.	6.
2.	7.
3.	8.
4.	9.
5.	10.

© Scott Foresman 3

Notes for Home: Your child read a story and used details to visualize its characters. ***Home Activity:*** Describe in detail a place you went or something interesting you saw today. Have your child draw a picture to show what he or she has visualized from your description.

Vocabulary

Directions: Choose the word from the box that best completes each sentence. Write the word on the line to the left.

Check the Words You Know

__ flushed
__ hurled
__ pronounced
__ refrigerator
__ sauce
__ success

____________________ **1.** My brother ran into the house and _____ his bag into the closet.

____________________ **2.** He came in after the game, and his face was _____.

____________________ **3.** He _____ one word, "Hot."

____________________ **4.** I got him some ice cream and topped it with chocolate _____.

____________________ **5.** I looked in the _____ and found him a jug of water too.

Directions: Choose the word from the box that best answers each clue. Write the word on the line to the left.

____________________ **6.** Food is stored inside this so that it will stay cold.

____________________ **7.** If you pour this on food, the food will taste better.

____________________ **8.** The outfielder did this with the baseball.

____________________ **9.** Your face did this when you were embarrassed.

____________________ **10.** When you win something, you have this.

Write a Recipe

On a separate sheet of paper, create a recipe for a new dish. List ingredients and tell how to prepare it. Use as many vocabulary words as you can.

A Sundae Success
1 scoop of ice cream
1 banana, cut up
2 tbl. chocolate sauce
1 swirl of whipped cream
1 cherry

© Scott Foresman 3

Notes for Home: Your child identified and used new vocabulary words from "The Extra-Good Sunday." ***Home Activity:*** Make up a story about cooking with your child. Use as many of the vocabulary words as possible. Work together to illustrate the story.

Name ______________________________________

Visualizing

- **To visualize** is to create a picture in your mind.
- When you read, use the details in the text along with what you know about the subject to see, smell, hear, taste, and feel what the author describes.

Directions: Reread what happens in "The Extra-Good Sunday" when Ramona and Beezus cook dinner. Then answer the questions below.

Grit, grit, grit sounded under the girls' feet. It was amazing how a tiny bit of spilled Cream of Wheat could make the entire kitchen floor gritty. At last their dinner was served, the dining-room light turned off, dinner announced, and the cooks, tense with anxiety that was hidden by candlelight, fell into their chairs as their parents seated themselves. Was this dinner going to be edible?

"Candles!" exclaimed Mrs. Quimby. "What a festive meal!"

"Let's taste it before we decide," said Mr. Quimby with his most wicked grin.

The girls watched anxiously as their father took his first bite of chicken. He chewed thoughtfully and said with more surprise than necessary, "Why this is good!"

From "The Extra-Good Sunday" from RAMONA QUIMBY, AGE 8 by Beverly Cleary. Copyright © 1981 by Beverly Cleary. By permission of Morrow Junior Books, a division of William Morrow & Company, Inc.

1. What can you hear in the kitchen? ______________________________

____

2. What can you see in the dining room? ___________________________

____

3. How do you picture Ramona's and Beezus's faces look while they wait for their parents to taste the meal?

____

4. How do you think Mr. Quimby's face looks after he tastes the chicken?

____

5. Pick another scene in the story. Describe on a separate sheet of paper what you visualize when you read.

© Scott Foresman 3

Notes for Home: Your child used details from the story to visualize a scene. ***Home Activity:*** Read a favorite story. Have your child point out the details of the story that help him or her picture what is happening.

Name ________________________________

Test-Taking Tips

1. Write your name on the test.
2. Read the directions carefully. Make sure you know exactly what you are supposed to do.
3. Read the question twice. Make sure you understand what the question is asking.
4. Read the answer choices for the question. Eliminate choices that do not make sense.
5. Mark your answer carefully.
6. Check your answer. Make sure that it makes the most sense out of all the answer choices.
7. If you have difficulty answering a question, you may want to go on to the next question. You can come back to difficult questions later.
8. If you finish the test early, go back and check all your answers.

© Scott Foresman 3

Name ______________________

Selection Test

Directions: Choose the best answer to each item. Mark the space for the answer you have chosen.

Part 1: Vocabulary

Find the answer choice that means about the same as the underlined word in each sentence.

1. The doctor pronounced her cured.
- wrote a sentence
- worried
- could not wait for
- stated something to be so

2. The trip was a success.
- big adventure
- good result
- unknown mystery
- long event

3. The cook was so warm, his face was flushed.
- pink
- tired
- clean
- dirty

4. Tyler hurled the ball.
- found
- picked up
- dropped
- threw

5. Nisha opened the refrigerator.
- container for carrying food
- kind of dessert
- thing that keeps food cold
- machine that chops food

6. The sauce was cold.
- a liquid served on food
- breeze
- a drink made from fruit
- pond

Part 2: Comprehension

Use what you know about the story to answer each item.

7. On Sunday morning, everyone in the Quimby family was—
- silent and grumpy.
- loud and silly.
- angry and noisy.
- pleasant and polite.

8. When Ramona got her skates out, her father told her that—
- it was going to rain soon.
- she was forgetting dinner.
- it was time for lunch.
- Mary Jane had called.

© Scott Foresman 3

GO ON

9. Which sentence about the girls making dinner best helps you see the scene in your mind?
- ⬭ "There must have been a special on yogurt."
- ⬭ "Ramona successfully broke the egg and tossed the shell onto the counter."
- ⬭ "Both girls spoke in whispers."
- ⬭ "The corn bread should bake at 400 degrees."

10. What is true about the cornbread and chicken that the girls make?
- ⬭ Both have unusual ingredients.
- ⬭ Both are overcooked.
- ⬭ Both have red specks.
- ⬭ Both taste awful.

11. Which detail best helps you see in your mind the scene when the girls prepare the chicken?
- ⬭ "'I can't stand touching raw meat,' she said."
- ⬭ "Beezus found a pair of kitchen tongs."
- ⬭ "Ramona remembered that the specks were red."
- ⬭ "They played tug-of-war with each thigh, leaving a sad-looking heap of skins on the counter."

12. The girls' biggest problem in making dinner is trying to—
- ⬭ find the recipes.
- ⬭ get all the dishes ready at the same time.
- ⬭ learn how to use the oven.
- ⬭ reach the ingredients they need.

13. Before he tries the food, Mr. Quimby thinks it will be—
- ⬭ uncooked.
- ⬭ delicious.
- ⬭ too hot.
- ⬭ not very tasty.

14. Why is this an "extra-good Sunday" for the Quimbys?
- ⬭ Everyone is happy again.
- ⬭ The meal is very good.
- ⬭ The girls go out skating.
- ⬭ The day ends up sunny.

15. The next time Beezus and Ramona have a difficult job to do, they probably will—
- ⬭ work together to get it done.
- ⬭ try at first but then give up.
- ⬭ get angry and refuse to do it.
- ⬭ pay a friend to do it for them.

STOP

© Scott Foresman 3

Name ______________________________

Generalizing

REVIEW

Directions: Read the story. Then read each question about the story. Choose the best answer to the question. Mark the space for the answer you have chosen.

Bake Sale

Almost everyone in Mrs. Kennedy's class was excited about this year's bake sale. This time, it was Gary's dad's turn to help the children bake. Once again, Mrs. Kennedy had dressed for the occasion. She wore a chef's hat.

All the children lined up outside the school kitchen except for Seth. He had never baked before. He was sure that whatever he made would be awful. He had volunteered to wash dishes the whole time, but Mrs. Kennedy said he should try to bake something. Seth wished he hadn't agreed.

The children got busy right away. They worked as a team and in no time they had batter and dough ready to cook. Even Seth smiled when he tasted the brownie batter he had helped make. It was delicious. Seth now knew that baking could be fun.

1. _____ of the children were excited about the bake sale.

- ⬭ All
- ⬭ A few
- ⬭ Most
- ⬭ None

2. It is most likely true that Mrs. Kennedy wears—

- ⬭ the same hat all the time.
- ⬭ only dresses.
- ⬭ lots of hats.
- ⬭ special clothes for special occasions.

3. It is most likely true that—

- ⬭ parents had helped with other bake sales.
- ⬭ this was the first time a parent helped with a bake sale.
- ⬭ Gary's dad always helped.
- ⬭ Seth's dad never helped.

4. It is most likely true that Seth—

- ⬭ would never be a good baker.
- ⬭ is always willing to try something new.
- ⬭ would never bake again.
- ⬭ would bake again.

5. What can you generalize from Seth's experience?

- ⬭ It can be fun to try new things.
- ⬭ Never try anything new.
- ⬭ Everyone likes to bake.
- ⬭ All baked goods taste delicious.

© Scott Foresman 3

Notes for Home: Your child made generalizations about a story. ***Home Activity:*** Read a short story with your child. Have your child point out clue words *(all, most, often, usually, never, sometimes)* that will help him or her make generalizations about the story.

Phonics: Vowel Digraphs *aw, au*; /ȯ/ Spelled *al*

Directions: Cross out the eight words in the box that do **not** have the vowel sound you hear in **talk.** Use the words that are left to complete the sentences.

all
because
blunder
cereal
fault
low
sauce
powder
raw
small
soak
strawberry
thaw
uncooked
vanilla
what

_______________ **1.** The chicken isn't cooked! It's still _____!

_______________ **2.** I'm to blame! It's all my _____!

_______________ **3.** It was frozen. I should have let it _____!

_______________ **4.** Let's eat dessert first! We can have ice cream with raspberry _____.

_______________ **5.** I just want a _____ amount. I want to leave room for the chicken!

_______________ **6.** Oh no! It's _____ flavored ice cream!

_______________ **7.** I can't eat it _____ I'm allergic to it.

_______________ **8.** I'm sorry, but it's _____ that I could find.

Directions: Cross out the words that do **not** have the vowel sound in **talk.**

9. chalk	coat	crawl
10. awful	autumn	asleep
11. hawk	hack	hall
12. dam	drawing	daughter
13. caught	claw	close
14. full	fault	fall
15. straw	shout	sausage

© Scott Foresman 3

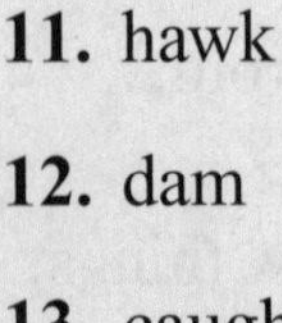

Notes for Home: Your child reviewed the vowel sound in *talk,* spelled *au, aw,* and *al* as in author, awful, and walk. ***Home Activity:*** Challenge your child to write words with these endings: *-all, -alk, -alt, -aught, -aw, -awl,* and *-awn.*

Name ______________________________

Phonics: The Schwa Sound

REVIEW

Directions: Read each sentence. Say the word with the underlined letter or letters in each sentence. Choose the word that has the same vowel sound as the word with the underlined letter or letters. Mark the space for the answer you have chosen.

1. Billy avoided the puddle.
- apple
- handed
- about
- tray

2. Emily read a magazine.
- senator
- rag
- grain
- gaze

3. Melissa fed the chickens.
- keep
- cheese
- happen
- pine

4. There are a lot of people here.
- let
- smallest
- leap
- mumble

5. Who came in second place?
- out
- apron
- loop
- hoping

6. Hand me the other piece.
- tooth
- short
- obey
- observe

7. Enter through this door.
- weather
- angry
- earring
- tent

8. Mom needs to put fuel in the car.
- label
- leap
- lent
- fumes

9. Greg climbed down the canyon.
- crayon
- yard
- hot
- you

10. Where are the children hiding?
- read
- often
- dine
- winning

© Scott Foresman 3

Notes for Home: Your child reviewed words with the schwa sound, an indistinct vowel sound heard in unstressed syllables such as *avoided.* ***Home Activity:*** Work with your child to find other words that begin with *a* that have the schwa sound, such as *again, above,* or *about.*

Name ____________________

Thesaurus

A **thesaurus** is a kind of dictionary that contains synonyms (words that have the same or similar meanings) and antonyms (words that have opposite meanings).

Directions: Read the thesaurus entry. Use the entry to answer the questions.

Entry Word ↓ **Definition** ↓

Synonyms →

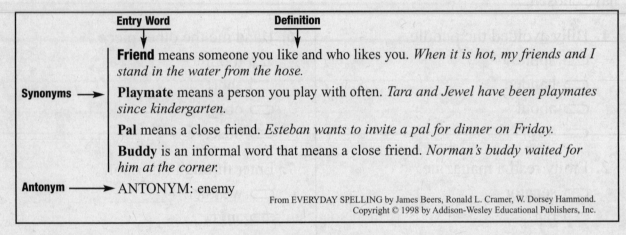

Friend means someone you like and who likes you. *When it is hot, my friends and I stand in the water from the hose.*

Playmate means a person you play with often. *Tara and Jewel have been playmates since kindergarten.*

Pal means a close friend. *Esteban wants to invite a pal for dinner on Friday.*

Buddy is an informal word that means a close friend. *Norman's buddy waited for him at the corner.*

Antonym → ANTONYM: enemy

From EVERYDAY SPELLING by James Beers, Ronald L. Cramer, W. Dorsey Hammond. Copyright © 1998 by Addison-Wesley Educational Publishers, Inc.

1. What is the entry word for this thesaurus entry? ____________________

2. What words could you use instead of *friend* in the following sentence? *My friend Cindy and I went swimming at the pond.*

____

3. What word or words could you use to replace the underlined phrase in the following sentence? *A frog is <u>not a friend</u> of the fly.*

____

4. How could you use a thesaurus to find words that have a similar meaning to *enemy?*

____

____

5. Why would a thesaurus be helpful when writing? Explain.

____

____

Notes for Home: Your child answered questions about a thesaurus entry. ***Home Activity:*** Help your child write a story. Encourage your child to replace some of the words by finding synonyms in a thesaurus. Read the story aloud to see if it sounds more interesting.

© Scott Foresman 3

Name ______________________________

Plot

- **Plot** includes the important events of a story that happen in the beginning, middle, and end, and how those events happen.
- Events that are important to the plot help keep the story going.

Directions: Reread "A Moon Landing." Complete the story map. List five important events that take place in the beginning, middle, and end of the story.

Story Section	Important Story Events
Beginning	**1.**
Middle	They put on their spacesuits and go outside.
	2.
	3.
End	**4.**
	5.

© Scott Foresman 3

Notes for Home: Your child read a story and identified important events in it. ***Home Activity:*** Challenge your child to tell you a story about himself or herself. Remind him or her to include a beginning, middle, and end.

Vocabulary

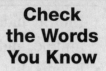

Directions: Draw a line to match each word with its definition.

1. unusual	to push into the air
2. astronaut	not common
3. weighed	world
4. launch	a member of a spacecraft crew
5. emergency	measured how heavy something is
6. globe	a sudden need for quick action

Check the Words You Know

__ astronaut
__ emergency
__ globe
__ launch
__ unusual
__ weighed

Directions: Choose the word from the box that best completes each sentence. Write the word on the line to the left.

__________________ **7.** My name is Chan. I work in space. I'm an _____.

__________________ **8.** Yesterday I climbed into my spaceship, got ready to _____, and took off.

__________________ **9.** From space I looked back at a swirling _____ of green and blue—Earth!

__________________ **10.** I'm lucky to be able to see such an _____ sight.

Write a Science Fiction Story

On a separate sheet of paper, write a short story in which you are an astronaut going to the moon. Use as many vocabulary words as you can.

© Scott Foresman 3

Notes for Home Your child identified and used new vocabulary words from *Floating Home*. ***Home Activity:*** Look up each vocabulary word in the dictionary. Read the definition aloud to your child. Challenge him or her to name the word.

Name ______________________________

Plot

- **Plot** includes the important events of a story that happen in the beginning, middle, and end, and how those events happen.
- Events that are important to the plot help keep the story going.

Directions: Reread the beginning of *Floating Home* and answer the first question below. Then reread the rest of the story and answer the other questions.

When Mrs. Selinsky asked the class to look at their homes in a new way and draw what they saw, Maxine left school and kept on walking. . . .

Artist's pad under her arm, her unsharpened colored pencils in their box, and a globe sharpener with all the countries of the world in her overalls pocket, Maxine passed her own home and kept on walking.

She was going to draw the most unusual picture of all, a picture of the Earth from space. She was going to be the youngest astronaut of all time!

From FLOATING HOME by David Getz. Text © 1997 by David Getz.
Reprinted by permission of Henry Holt and Company, LLC.

1. What important event happens in the beginning of the story?

____

____

____

2.–4. What important events happen in the middle of the story? Name three of these events.

____

____

____

____

5. On a separate sheet of paper, tell what happens at the end of the story.

© Scott Foresman 3

Notes for Home: Your child identified important events in a story. ***Home Activity:*** Watch a TV program with your child. Have your child describe the important events that happened in the beginning, middle, and end of the program.

Test-Taking Tips

1. Write your name on the test.
2. Read the directions carefully. Make sure you know exactly what you are supposed to do.
3. Read the question twice. Make sure you understand what the question is asking.
4. Read the answer choices for the question. Eliminate choices that do not make sense.
5. Mark your answer carefully.
6. Check your answer. Make sure that it makes the most sense out of all the answer choices.
7. If you have difficulty answering a question, you may want to go on to the next question. You can come back to difficult questions later.
8. If you finish the test early, go back and check all your answers.

© Scott Foresman 3

Name ______________________________

Selection Test

Directions: Choose the best answer to each item. Mark the space for the answer you have chosen.

Part 1: Vocabulary

Find the answer choice that means about the same as the underlined word in each sentence.

1. The music was unusual.
- ⬭ beautiful
- ⬭ not common
- ⬭ loud
- ⬭ enjoyed by many

2. The astronaut spoke on TV.
- ⬭ person who travels into space
- ⬭ person who reports the news
- ⬭ member of the government
- ⬭ person who teaches in school

3. I studied the globe.
- ⬭ star
- ⬭ small rocket
- ⬭ plan
- ⬭ model of the world

4. This is emergency food.
- ⬭ good tasting
- ⬭ for a time of sudden need
- ⬭ made with eggs
- ⬭ new and very popular

5. The dog weighed too much.
- ⬭ measured in pounds
- ⬭ barked at strangers
- ⬭ ran away
- ⬭ pulled on its leash

6. We watched Mom launch the model airplane.
- ⬭ send into the air
- ⬭ paint
- ⬭ glue together
- ⬭ pick up from the ground

Part 2: Comprehension

Use what you know about the story to answer each item.

7. Who gives Maxine the idea to look at her home in a new way?
- ⬭ an astronaut
- ⬭ her father
- ⬭ her art teacher
- ⬭ a reporter

8. How is life in the space shuttle different from life on Earth?
- ⬭ People don't get hungry.
- ⬭ Everything feels heavier.
- ⬭ You cannot hear anything.
- ⬭ There is no up or down.

9. Where is Maxine when she takes her last shower for two weeks?
- ⬭ at the Kennedy Space Center
- ⬭ at school
- ⬭ inside the space shuttle
- ⬭ at home

© Scott Foresman 3

GO ON

10. In the middle part of this story, Maxine—
- ⬭ sees a shooting star.
- ⬭ looks down at Earth.
- ⬭ sees her classmates drawing their houses.
- ⬭ listens to the countdown.

11. The ending of this story is mostly about Maxine's—
- ⬭ view of Earth.
- ⬭ return to Earth.
- ⬭ picture of her house.
- ⬭ letter to her parents.

12. Which of these events happened last?
- ⬭ The shuttle started to vibrate.
- ⬭ The ride got very smooth and quiet.
- ⬭ Maxine felt invisible hands pushing her back in her seat.
- ⬭ The cabin lit up from the fire and smoke outside the windows.

13. Which sentence best describes Maxine?
- ⬭ She does not like school.
- ⬭ She has a great imagination.
- ⬭ She wants to be a reporter.
- ⬭ She is lazy most of the time.

14. Which part of this story is fantasy?
- ⬭ An eight-year-old girl rides in the space shuttle.
- ⬭ Astronauts travel into space.
- ⬭ A girl has a globe pencil sharpener.
- ⬭ Students look at their homes in new ways.

15. What is the most exciting part of the trip for Maxine?
- ⬭ taking a shower
- ⬭ putting on a space suit
- ⬭ seeing Earth from space
- ⬭ climbing into the space shuttle

STOP

© Scott Foresman 3

Setting and Steps in a Process

REVIEW

Directions: Read the story. Then read each question about the story. Choose the best answer to the question. Mark the space for the answer you have chosen.

Preparing for a Trip to Space

The astronauts at the space command center were getting ready for their trip into space. They had spent months learning how to operate the space shuttle.

Then they had their medical tests to make sure they were healthy. Next, the astronauts had their pressure suits adjusted to fit them. Then they wore their suits in the Anti-Gravity Chamber to get used to being without gravity.

The day before their trip, the technicians checked the space shuttle. Then the astronauts prepared their equipment. The shuttle was also packed with the food they would need. The astronauts woke up early the next day. They put on their suits, waved to the crowds, and stepped into the space shuttle. They were ready for their trip.

1. This story takes place—
- in space.
- a long time ago.
- at a space command center.
- on a distant planet.

2. First, the astronauts—
- go in the Anti-Gravity Chamber.
- wave to the crowds.
- put on their suits.
- learn how to operate the shuttle.

3. After the technicians checked the space shuttle, the astronauts—
- fixed a broken part.
- walked into the shuttle.
- ate.
- prepared their equipment.

4. The first thing the astronauts did the day of the trip was—
- wake up early.
- have their medical tests.
- wave to the crowds.
- step into the space shuttle.

5. The last thing the astronauts did the day of the trip was—
- wake up early.
- have their medical tests.
- wave to the crowds.
- step into the space shuttle.

© Scott Foresman 3

Notes for Home: Your child read a story and identified its setting and the steps in a process. ***Home Activity:*** With your child, review a step-by-step process such as a recipe or game directions. Together, follow the steps in order.

Name ________________________________

Phonics: Vowel Digraphs *ui, ew*

Directions: Write **ui** or **ew** to complete each word. Write the whole word on the line to the left.

______________ **1.** The plane fl___ Mark to the space center.

______________ **2.** Mark drank some orange j___ce in the center's cafeteria.

______________ **3.** He ate a big bowl of st___.

______________ **4.** Then he had fr___t salad for dessert.

______________ **5.** He watched the n___ space shuttle take off.

______________ **6.** It gr___ smaller and smaller as it rose.

______________ **7.** He dr___ a picture of it taking off.

______________ **8.** The school n___spaper printed his picture.

______________ **9.** Later, he got to try on a space s___t.

Directions: Cross out all the words in the box that do **not** have the same vowel sound as **fruit** and **new.** Write the remaining words in the correct column.

ui as in fruit

10. ______________

11. ______________

12. ______________

13. ______________

ew as in new

14. ______________

15. ______________

16. ______________

17. ______________

18. ______________

19. ______________

20. ______________

suit	grew
juice	news
few	great
slice	grow
chew	push
bruise	air
brunch	crew
stew	cruise
quiet	dew

© Scott Foresman 3

Notes for Home: Your child reviewed words with *ui* and *ew* that have the same vowel sounds, such as in *juice* and *stew*. ***Home Activity:*** Help your child list other words with *ui* and *ew* that have this same vowel sound.

Name ____________________

Word Study: Syllabication

REVIEW

Directions: Read each sentence. Say the underlined word in each sentence. Choose the word that has the same number of syllables as the underlined word. Mark the space for the answer you have chosen.

1. Mom unpacked the suitcase.
- ⬭ recovered
- ⬭ packed
- ⬭ unwrap
- ⬭ wrapped

2. Richard lost his sunglasses.
- ⬭ basket
- ⬭ newspaper
- ⬭ remembering
- ⬭ sunset

3. The atmosphere around Venus is cloudy.
- ⬭ attention
- ⬭ airplane
- ⬭ weather
- ⬭ above

4. The crewmates boarded the shuttle.
- ⬭ friends
- ⬭ partners
- ⬭ astronauts
- ⬭ mechanics

5. Harry removed his jacket.
- ⬭ ripped
- ⬭ lost
- ⬭ washed
- ⬭ unzipped

6. I could feel the plane's vibrations.
- ⬭ elastic
- ⬭ nation
- ⬭ building
- ⬭ driver

7. The captain lead the crew.
- ⬭ trapped
- ⬭ cape
- ⬭ babysitter
- ⬭ poster

8. She rested after the game.
- ⬭ jumped
- ⬭ walked
- ⬭ waited
- ⬭ ran

9. Marik looked at the calendar.
- ⬭ date
- ⬭ silver
- ⬭ early
- ⬭ comforter

10. Bailey discovered a new star.
- ⬭ distance
- ⬭ repainted
- ⬭ covered
- ⬭ undone

© Scott Foresman 3

Notes for Home: Your child identified the number of syllables in a word. ***Home Activity:*** Write two- and three-syllable words on index cards. Have your child say each word and sort the cards by the number of syllables.

Name ______________________________

Newspaper

A **newspaper** is a daily or weekly publication that contains factual news stories, entertaining feature stories, advertisements, editorials that express opinions, and other useful information, such as TV listings.

Directions: Identify the different newspaper parts by writing **advertisement, editorial, news,** or **sports** on the lines. Then answer the question below.

Glendale News

April 7, 2005 | Vol. 12, Issue 14

1. ______________________________

Local Girl Wins Trip

by Kira Jones

Jennifer Myers, a student at Glendale High School, will be traveling next month to Cape Canaveral to visit the NASA space station. Ms. Myers won the trip by writing an essay about why space exploration is important to our future.

2. ______________________________

TERRY'S TERRIFIC TOYS

Customer Appreciation Day

Wednesday, December 9

Stores will be open until midnight.

Take $5.00 off any purchase.

3. ______________________________

Soccer Match Rescheduled

by Jim Brentwood

Last night's soccer match between the Glendale Rockets and the Midvale Moonbeams was canceled due to the rain. The game has been rescheduled for next Thursday at 5:00 P.M. This gives Rockets forward Chris Cooper more time to heal his sprained ankle.

4. ______________________________

Letters to the Editor

Dear Editor,

I just came back from a visit to the National Air and Space Museum. The tour was informative and interesting. Thanks for highlighting this great museum in your travel section!

Marco Martinez

5. How can you use headlines to help you find interesting articles to read?

____

Notes for Home: Your child identified the different parts of a newspaper. ***Home Activity:*** Look through a local newspaper with your child. Help him or her to identify the different sections of the paper and scan the headlines to find interesting articles to read.

© Scott Foresman 3

Name ________________________________

Realism and Fantasy

- A **realistic story** tells about something that could happen in real life.
- A **fantasy** has some things that could not possibly happen. Some also have things that could happen.

Directions: Reread "Ali and the Snake" and "Verdi Wonders." Then complete each table. Write **Yes** if the story event could happen in real life. Write **No** if the story event could not possibly happen. Finally, tell whether each story is realistic or a fantasy.

Ali and the Snake

Story Event	Yes or No?
A man from the zoo brings a snake, Silvia, to Ali's school.	**1.**
Silvia is brown, yellow, and orange.	**2.**
Ali volunteers to hold Silvia.	**3.**
She wears Silvia around her neck, her arms, and her ankles.	**4.**
Is this story realistic or a fantasy? Explain. **5.**	

Verdi Wonders

Story Event	Yes or No?
The mother python sends hatchlings into the forest.	**6.**
The mother python speaks to the hatchlings.	**7.**
Verdi wonders why he should hurry up and grow big and green.	**8.**
Verdi goes looking for older snakes to talk to him.	**9.**
Is this story realistic or a fantasy? Explain. **10.**	

© Scott Foresman 3

Notes for Home: Your child identified story events that could really happen and those that could not really happen. ***Home Activity:*** Read a story with your child. Have your child explain whether the story is a realistic story or a fantasy and how he or she knows.

Vocabulary

Directions: Choose a word from the box that best replaces the underlined word or words. Write the word on the line.

Check the Words You Know
__ blinding
__ crystal
__ echoing
__ ledge
__ remarkable
__ scout
__ sparkling
__ treasure

______________ **1.** My family had an unusual experience when we went hiking.

______________ **2.** While walking along the trail, my sister looked into a cave near a narrow shelf.

______________ **3.** Inside the small cave she saw something that seemed to be glittering.

______________ **4.** My sister yelled loudly, which caused a strange repeating sound in the cave.

______________ **5.** "Quick," she said. "I think I've found a valuable thing!"

Directions: Choose the word from the box that best matches each clue. Write the word on the line.

______________ **6.** Both snow and sugar are examples of this.

______________ **7.** This person is sent ahead of others to find or look for something.

______________ **8.** This rhymes with *measure* and is worth a lot.

______________ **9.** You wouldn't want to step off this.

______________ **10.** This is what you call sunlight that is too bright.

Write a Journal Entry

On a separate sheet of paper, write a journal entry of a day spent treasure hunting with your family. Use as many vocabulary words as you can.

Notes for Home: Your child identified and used new vocabulary words from the story *Two Bad Ants. **Home Activity:*** Together, create a play about the adventures of two ants. Act out your play, using as many vocabulary words as possible.

© Scott Foresman 3

Name ______________________

Realism and Fantasy

- A **realistic story** tells about something that could happen in real life.
- A **fantasy** has some things that could not possibly happen. Some also have things that could happen.

Directions: Reread the section in *Two Bad Ants* where the ants find the crystals. Then answer the questions below.

They crossed smooth shiny surfaces, then followed the scout up a glassy, curved wall. They had reached their goal. From the top of the wall they looked below to a sea of crystals. One by one the ants climbed down into the sparkling treasure.

Quickly they each chose a crystal, then turned to start the journey home. There was something about this unnatural place that made the ants nervous. In fact, they left in such a hurry that none of them noticed the two small ants who stayed behind.

"Why go back?" one asked the other. "This place may not feel like home, but look at all these crystals."

"You're right," said the other, "we can stay here and eat this tasty treasure every day forever."

From TWO BAD ANTS. Copyright © 1988 by Chris Van Allsburg. Reprinted by permission of Houghton Mifflin Company. All rights reserved.

1. The ants crawl up a kitchen sink. Could this event really happen? Explain.

____

2. The ants climb into the sea of crystals (sugar). Could this event really happen? Explain.

____

3. The ants each carry away a sugar crystal. Could this event really happen? Explain.

____

4. The two small ants stay behind and talk to each other. Could this event really happen? Explain.

____

5. Is *Two Bad Ants* a realistic story or a fantasy? Write your explanation on a separate sheet of paper.

© Scott Foresman 3

Notes for Home: Your child identified story events that could happen in real life and story events that could not possibly happen. ***Home Activity:*** Together, make up a realistic story or a fantasy. Take turns saying sentences until the story ends.

Name ____________________________________

Test-Taking Tips

1. Write your name on the test.
2. Read the directions carefully. Make sure you know exactly what you are supposed to do.
3. Read the question twice. Make sure you understand what the question is asking.
4. Read the answer choices for the question. Eliminate choices that do not make sense.
5. Mark your answer carefully.
6. Check your answer. Make sure that it makes the most sense out of all the answer choices.
7. If you have difficulty answering a question, you may want to go on to the next question. You can come back to difficult questions later.
8. If you finish the test early, go back and check all your answers.

© Scott Foresman 3

Selection Test

Directions: Choose the best answer to each item. Mark the space for the answer you have chosen.

Part 1: Vocabulary

Find the answer choice that means about the same as the underlined word in each sentence.

1. Jon stood on the <u>ledge</u>.
   - chair
   - narrow shelf
   - ladder
   - brick wall

2. The bells were <u>echoing</u> loudly.
   - cracking
   - hitting together
   - falling
   - repeating a sound

3. We found a <u>treasure</u>.
   - large book
   - something cold
   - something valuable
   - deep well

4. The light was <u>blinding</u>.
   - making unable to see
   - very thin
   - having a red color
   - not bright

5. Is that a <u>crystal</u>?
   - window
   - small piece of something, such as sugar
   - open door
   - round object, such as a ball

6. That is <u>remarkable</u> news!
   - awful
   - bringing joy
   - having just happened
   - worth noting; unusual

7. Her ring was <u>sparkling</u>.
   - shining
   - purple
   - pretty
   - small

8. The <u>scout</u> came back to the tent.
   - heavy truck
   - person who puts out fires
   - person or thing sent to find something
   - animal that guards something

© Scott Foresman 3

GO ON

Name ______________________________

Part 2: Comprehension

Use what you know about the story to answer each item.

9. The ants wanted to gather more crystals to—
- make their queen happy.
- build a new nest.
- fill a cup.
- make the water sweet.

10. You can tell from this story that ants have to—
- eat all the time.
- stay away from fireflies.
- drink lots of water.
- watch out for spiders.

11. The "mountain" that the ants climb is a—
- shoe.
- wall.
- car.
- book.

12. Which part of this story is fantasy?
- Ants go into a house.
- Ants leave their home.
- Ants talk to each other.
- Ants go out at night.

13. When the two ants are in the brown liquid, the "cave" they see is a—
- cup.
- spoon.
- toaster.
- person's mouth.

14. What did the whole group of ants find most strange about being inside the house?
- The water was cold.
- There were no spiders.
- The sky was gone.
- It was warm inside.

15. How were the two ants in this story "bad"?
- They stayed out all night and did not do their jobs.
- They talked back to their queen.
- They tried to eat an English muffin.
- They took crystals that did not belong to them.

STOP

© Scott Foresman 3

Name ______________________________

REVIEW

Making Judgments

Directions: Read the beginning of the story. Then read each question about the story. Choose the best answer to the question. Mark the space for the answer you have chosen.

Curious Alice

Every summer Alice's whole family got together at Uncle Joe's farm. The first day was always fun. Alice liked to catch up on family news with her cousins.

However, on the second day, the games began. The whole family was divided into teams, and they would play sports. Alice didn't like running and she wasn't very good at throwing a ball, so she didn't always have fun.

This year, Alice decided to skip the games and explore the farm. She was so curious about the cows that she opened the gate to get a closer look. As she did, one of the cows escaped.

Luckily, Uncle Joe was able to catch the cow and return it safely to the pen. Alice was sorry, and she promised not to wander off again. Uncle Joe accepted her apology and said he would try to organize a game that wasn't a sport.

1. At a family reunion, Alice would most likely enjoy—
- talking with her cousins.
- playing baseball.
- playing tag.
- writing poems.

2. How do you think Alice feels when the family plays sports?
- unhappy
- tired
- happy
- relieved

3. Alice's actions show that she—
- is a mean person.
- is easily bored.
- always causes trouble.
- doesn't always think about what she is doing.

4. Uncle Joe's actions show that he—
- is kind and understanding.
- doesn't like young people.
- is unkind.
- is unforgiving.

5. Why do you think Alice promises not to wander off again?
- She doesn't like to be alone.
- She doesn't want to cause trouble again.
- She doesn't enjoy sports.
- She doesn't like cows.

© Scott Foresman 3

Notes for Home: Your child used information in a story to make judgments about its characters. ***Home Activity:*** Read a story with your child. Ask your child to make judgments about how the characters act.

Name ______________________________

Word Study: Affixes

Directions: Add a prefix or a suffix to each base word below to build a new word. Remember, you may need to drop an **e** or change a **y** to **i** before adding a suffix. Write the new word on the line.

Add a Prefix	Add a Suffix
1. un- + aware = ____________	**6.** power + -ful = ____________
2. un- + happy = ____________	**7.** hope + -less = ____________
3. re- + appear = ____________	**8.** taste + -y = ____________
4. dis- + honest = ____________	**9.** final + -ly = ____________
5. dis- + trust = ____________	**10.** fever + -ish = ____________

Directions: Write the prefix, base word, and suffix for each word below.

Word	Prefix	Base Word	Suffix
11. unwisely	____________	____________	____________
12. remarkable	____________	____________	____________
13. dishonestly	____________	____________	____________
14. unhappiness	____________	____________	____________
15. unbearably	____________	____________	____________
16. distasteful	____________	____________	____________
17. unlucky	____________	____________	____________
18. unkindness	____________	____________	____________
19. distrustful	____________	____________	____________
20. unhealthy	____________	____________	____________

Notes for Home: Your child worked with words containing prefixes and suffixes. ***Home Activity:*** Write the prefixes *un-, re-,* and *dis-* and the suffixes *-ful, -ness, -ly, -y, -able, -ably,* and *-ish* on slips of paper. Take turns choosing slips and saying words with these beginnings and endings.

© Scott Foresman 3

Name ______________________________

REVIEW

Phonics: Vowel Digraphs *aw, au;* /ȯ/ Spelled *al*

Directions: Read each sentence. Say the underlined word in each sentence. Choose the word that has the same vowel sound as the underlined word. Mark the space for the answer you have chosen.

1. Bill, did you see those ants on the wall?
- ⬭ sauce
- ⬭ way
- ⬭ climb
- ⬭ fingernails

2. Bill just yawned.
- ⬭ yard
- ⬭ loaned
- ⬭ lawn
- ⬭ towel

3. It was because he was tired.
- ⬭ hawk
- ⬭ can
- ⬭ bed
- ⬭ use

4. The ants crawled in the hole.
- ⬭ air
- ⬭ creep
- ⬭ grab
- ⬭ ball

5. The ants had fallen in the sugar.
- ⬭ flow
- ⬭ fault
- ⬭ flat
- ⬭ flapping

6. The ants climbed on the faucet.
- ⬭ fat
- ⬭ walk
- ⬭ wait
- ⬭ sink

7. Ants are very small.
- ⬭ saw
- ⬭ smell
- ⬭ melting
- ⬭ smile

8. You don't see many ants in autumn.
- ⬭ June
- ⬭ fall
- ⬭ April
- ⬭ May

9. My cat tried to catch one with his paw.
- ⬭ jar
- ⬭ pail
- ⬭ talk
- ⬭ two

10. But they escaped out to the lawn.
- ⬭ lane
- ⬭ loan
- ⬭ under
- ⬭ laundry

© Scott Foresman 3

Notes for Home: Your child chose words with *au, aw,* and *al* that have the same vowel sound *(sauce, jaw, ball).* ***Home Activity:*** Help your child write sentences that rhyme using words with this vowel sound.

Technology: Electronic Media

Electronic media includes computers (program software, CD-ROMs, Internet) and other media, such as audiotapes, videotapes, films, and television broadcasts.

Directions: Write **computer, audiotape, videotape,** or **television** to answer each question. Explain your answer.

1. For a school project, Mandy wants to compare the sounds of different kinds of birds. What type of electronic media should she use?

____

2. Jeremy is having a hard time remembering a series of positions for his martial arts class. He wants to see the same moves several times. Which type of electronic media should he use?

____

____

3. Miriam is writing a report on the different roles of bees in a bee hive. She wants to create a table showing this information in her report. Which type of electronic media should she use?

____

4. Ty is getting ready for school. He wants to know whether rain is expected today. Which type of electronic media should he use?

____

____

5. Describe a school project where you could use one of the electronic media listed above. Explain why this particular type of media is helpful.

____

____

____

Notes for Home: Your child decided which type of electronic media best suits each situation. ***Home Activity:*** Walk through your home and identify any electronic media you have. Discuss how he or she might use each kind of media for researching or studying.

© Scott Foresman 3

© Scott Foresman 3

Name ____________________

Reading Log

Date	What is the title?	Who is the author?	What did you think of it?

Name ______________________________

Reading Log

Date	What is the title?	Who is the author?	What did you think of it?

© Scott Foresman 3

© Scott Foresman 3

Name ____________________

Reading Log

Date	What is the title?	Who is the author?	What did you think of it?

Name ______________________________

Reading Log

Date	What is the title?	Who is the author?	What did you think of it?

© Scott Foresman 3

© Scott Foresman 3

Name ______________________________

Reading Log

Date	What is the title?	Who is the author?	What did you think of it?

Name ______________________________

Reading Log

Date	What is the title?	Who is the author?	What did you think of it?

© Scott Foresman 3